MW00426891

A Pocket Guide to Adidas
Josh Sims

Introduction

'There were many times when I was asked to create a performance shoe for the street, but my reaction was always, "We are Adidas. We are sport",' Jacques Chassaing would once say. 'I strongly believed that if I was going to create, [for example], a new tennis shoe, then first and foremost it should be a fantastic shoe to play tennis [in]. If the wearers all felt it was comfortable enough to be streetwear, then great, but only because they decided that. Not us.'

In these few lines Chassaing, arguably Adidas's most influential designer – quoted here in the monograph of his work, *From Soul to Sole* (2022) – summed up the guiding ethos of a company that was established in the wake of the Second World War, and which has roots stretching back over a century. For whatever sporting need it has addressed – and it would consider the most obscure of sports – Adidas has always pursued a philosophy of functionality first. Its shoes must be fit for purpose.

Once, Adidas was effectively alone. It didn't just pioneer technologies to improve the sporting experience of anyone in its shoes, it also pioneered what would become a gigantic global industry,

A Pocket Guide to Adidas

Josh Sims

Laurence King

Contents

with the years since the 1920s seeing the creation of numerous competitors, many of which – Nike, most obviously – creating their own famous designs.

They all owe a debt to Adidas, because – while it might not have been its intention – Adidas would also help to shape a culture in which sports shoes were worn, as Chassaing put it, 'for the street'. It's the stylistic by-product of the technology Adidas once deployed that, remarkably, has encouraged so many of its styles to continue to be worn decades after their creation. That's why Adidas can lay claim to so many iconic products, and to having found a place in the wardrobes of myriad diverse subcultures around the world.

Adidas has achieved all of this with, it might often seem, complete disinterest. Indeed, in its focused pursuit of utility over fashionability, in its regard for efficiency and order, this somewhat faceless corporation plays to many stereotypically German traits. But, of course, that detachment has only ever served to enhance its cool.

History

The story of Adidas begins with a bitter family dispute and ends with the creation of not one, but two global sportswear companies. As often happens, two brothers – in this case Adolf and Rudolf Dassler, of Herzogenaurach in Bavaria, Germany – found that they could no longer work together.

Herzogenaurach was a small town of just 4,000 people, with most of its biggest employers being in the shoemaking business. Adolf Dassler's father was employed by one of them and, perhaps

LEFT: Adidas advert from 2000s. The global brand has its origins in the 1920s.

aware of the need for his youngest son to make his own path, encouraged him to apprentice as a baker. This was barely completed when, aged 18, Adolf Dassler was drafted to serve in the German Army over the final months of the First World War. That, undoubtedly, gave him time to think.

By the war's end, and having returned to civilian life, Dassler concluded that his interest really lay in footwear. More specifically, sports footwear; more

ABOVE: Adolf
Dassler in the
1920s in the
Dassler Brothers
shoe factory.

particularly still, in the development of different kinds
of footwear for different sports – a revolutionary
idea at the time.

Consequently, putting both bakery and battle
behind him, Dassler teamed up with a local
shoemaker by the name of Karl Zech, opened
a small repair business in the washroom at the

back of the family home, and began to work on developing his design ideas. It was a family affair from the beginning: '[Adolf Dassler] started experimenting, manufacturing shoes in his mother's laundry room,' his youngest daughter Sigi Dassler would tell the BBC in 2022. 'He used all kinds of raw material he could find, including bread bags, and his father helped him to organize this, as well as build machines in order to get the business started.'

Yet it took a leap of the imagination to believe that a business could be made out of such a specialist product. In an economically crippled post-war Germany, materials were scarce and electricity supply so intermittent to the town that Dassler had to rig up a leather-milling machine to a stationary bicycle in order to generate their own power, pedalled by the fledging company's first employee, Josef Erhardt. There was also the question of who needed expensive track shoes at this time anyway?

But Dassler was persistent to the last. Much as he had not been enamoured of baking, so his older brother Rudolf was not so keen on being a policeman. In 1923 Adolf brought Rudolf into the business and the following year they launched Gebrüder Dassler Schuhfabrik, roughly translating as the Dassler Brothers Shoe Factory. Adolf focused on design and development, Rudolf on sales and marketing.

The Beginnings

The first two years were not easy: with a team of around twelve, the company produced just 50 pairs of shoes a day. But, crucially, these were 50 pairs of a kind that nobody else was making – the first football boots with leather studs and the first spiked track shoes. By the end of 1926 the company was making one hundred pairs a day. More pertinent to the credibility of its product, two years later, national sporting heroes were wearing Dassler's spikes, with runner Lina Radke bringing home a gold medal (and setting a new world record) at the Amsterdam Olympics.

Even with these early designs it was clear that Dassler was rethinking how construction methods and materials used to make a shoe could serve in the very particular needs of the athlete wearing it. His first sprint shoes had an upper made of very soft but thin – and so lightweight – goatskin; and its cleats were pitched at a bio-mechanically designed angle to the sole, as though the shoe was already in motion.

By 1928 Dassler shoes had one of the first screw-in spike systems, with each spike pushed through the prepunched outsole and then screwed into place using a hexagonal steel disc. They employed a riveted metal plate to stiffen the forefront and provide better pressure distribution between the spikes. Spikes would later be angled and of a length that worked best for the individual athlete. These ideas would be among Dassler's first patented designs.

The Olympic Pacesetters

Look at the feet and your eyes will convince you that more olympic athletes wear adidas than all other brands combined. The secret is that adidas makes the right shoe for the right event.

adidas® ◢◣◤

—the original 3-stripe shoe.

Success at the Amsterdam Olympics also reassured Adolf Dassler that his design ideas were right, and that they needed to be pushed harder. To this end, from the mid 1920s he teamed up with Josef Waitzer, a national track and field trainer with his eyes set on making waves at the forthcoming 1932 Los Angeles Olympics. Waitzer helped ensure that more athletes wore Dassler shoes on this world stage, while Dassler himself attended the Shoe Technical School in Pirmasens, Germany, with a view to testing the potential of some of his other ideas. It was there that he also met his future wife Käthe, the daughter of a leading shoemould manufacturer.

ABOVE: Advert from the 1970s. Adidas's success would lead to predominance at the Olympics in years to come.

Dassler saw the Olympics as a test of his products

But it would be the next Olympic Games in 1936 – in Berlin and so on home turf – that really offered the opportunity for Dassler shoes to make an impression. As a showcase for all things German, the Berlin Olympics was a huge marketing opportunity; here athletes from around the world were introduced to Dassler's products, notably its 'Geda' spikes. Dassler-shod athletes set two world and three Olympic

BELOW: The 1936 Olympics Stadium in Berlin.

records, and took home 17 medal wins, seven of them gold. It's likely that the legendary Jesse Owens was among those to wear Dassler.

Always looking for improvements, Dassler saw the Olympics as a test of his products too: Waitzer discovered, for example, that the spikes on one 100m runner's shoes were wearing out after being worn across hard paths around the Olympic village. 'We have to make the spikes a little stronger, even with the light sprinter shoes,'

BELOW: Jesse Owens at the 1936 Berlin Olympic Games.

he reported back, adding enthusiastically, 'I'm going to Bochum today where I'm meeting the best sprinters.' With Olympic success behind them, in 1938 the brothers were able to open a second factory and were soon producing around one thousand pairs of shoes a day, across eleven different sporting disciplines.

The Coming War

A period of great strain – both for the business and for Adolf and Rudolf's relationship – was just around the corner. In 1939 Germany was at war again, exports became severely restricted and consumer demand for sports footwear all but collapsed. The second factory was closed. Both Rudolf and Adolf were drafted to serve in the army, the latter for two years as a radio operator in the Luftwaffe. On his release from the military Adolf Dassler could get back to making shoes, and was ordered to complete an order for 10,500 pairs of sports shoes a year for the German Army.

Later much of the Dasslers' factory machinery was co-opted by the state to make anti-tank weapons for the military – as was the case for much manufacturing across the country. Both Dassler brothers had been members of the Nazi party since 1933 – a matter, it's been argued, of practical expediency, since business would otherwise have been severely hampered and the Dassler workforce jeopardized. It has also been surmised that Adolf Dassler saw membership as a means of supplying the Hitler Youth movement and so getting the local boys and girls into sport. Yet by then the rot had set in between the two brothers. Quite what lay at the root of an apparently deeply acrimonious split remains open to speculation, since it has never been properly understood. According to the Adi and Käthe Dassler Memorial Foundation, Rudolf was drafted for longer than Adolf and is reported to have questioned Adolf's ability to run the company in his absence, even though that was their agreement. Had Rudolf's attempt at micro-management from afar caused the rift? Certainly, Adolf declined Rudolf's request that his wife Friedl act on his behalf.

Still more rumours abound. Some have claimed that Rudolf had a part in the reallocation of the manufacturing plant from footwear to weaponry – under the management of the military – in order to expedite Adolf's own conscription, though this surely would have been a state-issued directive. Rudolf even claimed that Adolf was responsible for his year-long internment at the end of the war.

Others have suggested that Rudolf eventually went AWOL during his wartime service, and this was what led to his arrest by the Allies. Had that upset brother Adolf? And yet others have claimed that Rudolf was a womanizer. Had Adolf been jealous, or disapproving, or suspicious of some affair with Käthe? Understandably, none of this makes for good PR, and Adidas tends to avoid mention of its pre-war history altogether.

And yet, despite this rift – never healed – the Dassler business just about survived the war. Remarkably, when US troops occupying Germany set out to destroy the factory, Käthe Dassler managed to convince them that it only made footwear, after all. American troops – aware of Dassler's connection with Jesse Owens – even became enthusiastic customers. Indeed, from spring 1945 American officers were billeted in the Dassler family home, and they helped acquire surplus war materials – everything from tent canvas to rubber rafts – that could be radically repurposed to allow some kind of shoe production to start again.

Yet the Allied occupation of Germany was not without its cost: as a member of the Nazi Party, Adolf was in 1946 barred from owning a business, a penalty that he challenged, in part successfully – with a Jewish friend even testifying that Adolf had protected him during the war. Adolf was put on two years' probation and permitted to resume business under supervision. In early 1947 he was allowed to manage the company as owner once again. The following year – after years of turmoil and strife – the brothers finally decided to go their separate ways. Sadly, they never spoke again.

A New Era

In 1948 Rudolf Dassler founded the sportswear company Puma, also in Herzogenaurach. Adolf – or Adi, as he was more affectionately known – would, the following year, launch his company, Adolf Dassler Sportschuhfabrik, on the other side of town with around two-thirds of the original workforce. The story goes that the company was originally registered as 'Addas' – combining 'Ad' from Adolf with 'Das' from Dassler, but that was already in use by a maker of children's shoes. Adolf took the paperwork and scribbled in the letter 'i', making 'Adidas'.

The parting of ways didn't, however, heal the rift between Adolf and Rudolf: even employees of the two companies were not on speaking terms, frequenting different businesses in order to remain separated. Herzogenaurach was dubbed 'the town of bent necks', following the habit of residents to examine each other's footwear to see which camp they were in.

'We didn't even mention the name, Adidas, at home,' Michael Dassler, Rudolf Dassler's grandson, has said. 'We usually said N.G., for the German *nie gehort*, "never heard of it". It's like in *Harry Potter* – the name Voldemort, which is not mentioned.'

When it transpired that Adidas and Puma might end up in a crippling bidding war to sign the Brazilian football superstar Pelé, they entered into what they called the 'Pelé Pact', an informal agreement that neither of the companies would sign him. When Pelé bent down to tie his Puma boots during the 1970 World Cup – captured on TV for millions of viewers – Adolf was not best pleased. That event, as his daughter Sigi Dassler would note, only served to pour gasoline on the fire of the rivalry.

By now Adidas didn't have the market dominance Adolf and Rudolf had enjoyed in the 1920s and 1930s. Germany was undergoing its post-war reconstruction, and while the Allies were determined to help rebuild the German economy, competition for business was severe. One answer was innovation. Adidas already had a track record in developing spikes. Now it upped the ante.

The 1950s saw Adidas made great strides in certain sports – track and field and football especially – as well as set out the makings of its design pedigree through the creation of such shoe models as the Samba and the Italia. In 1952 Adidas also moved into clothing and sports equipment, producing products such as its own footballs. Three years later it opened its first factory outside of Germany, in France, under the management of Adolf and Käthe's son Horst, while their other children (four daughters), as well as Käthe's sister, all had senior roles in the company too.

Käthe Dassler became the social lubricant between the company and sports organizations, governing bodies and retailers, while Adi took a hands-on approach to trying as many sports as possible, together with undertaking countless interviews with elite athletes, all the better understand what made the right shoe for the right activity. That was his big idea: that sports footwear should be truly fit for its particular purpose. Until this point track athletes, for example, wore the same spikes for all events.

No activity was discounted. While Adidas soon became best known for its football boots, track and field and racquet sports shoes – that is, shoes for all the more mainstream sports – Dassler also developed specialist shoes, the first of their kind in

BELOW: British decathlete Daley Thompson wearing Adidas in 1980.

many instances, for the likes of bowling, skiing, fencing, boxing and shooting.

'There wasn't anything else [at that time],' recalled Willi Holdorf, the first German to win Olympic gold in decathlon, in 1964, and later a sales rep for Adidas. 'Then came high-jump spikes with the soles a bit thicker. Then I was into the decathlon, and I needed spikes for throwing the javelin. But [still] I did all of the running events with the same spikes. But then that changed too,' he said in papers held by the Adi and Käthe Dassler Memorial Foundation

RIGHT: Adidas prided itself on the design of shoes specific to the sports they were worn for.

BELOW: Adidas boxing boots.

Indeed, following Dassler's habit of taking a bespoke approach to supplying athletes with spikes, whenever possible, he provided Holdorf with a special pair for the 1,500m, built up at the heels to encourage the athlete to run more on his toes. 'I think that won me a few seconds, maybe even five,' Holdorf would claim. That shoe, called the Interval, would become an early bestseller. Likewise, Dassler made a one-off pair of padded boots that laced at the heel for the West German footballer Uwe Seeler, who suffered from Achilles tendonitis. These allowed the striker to play in the 1966 World Cup final against England.

When track surfaces were suddenly switched from cinder to synthetic shortly ahead of the 1968 Mexico City Olympics, Dassler was forced to adapt in kind. His competitors proposed the use of so-called brushes, even finer spikes that wouldn't get stuck in the new surface, but the Olympic authorities banned them as potentially dangerous. Dassler had his own idea. He devised a style of spikes that took the form of stubby triangular protrusions that didn't catch in or damage the surface but, crucially, still bit enough to give athletes traction.

According to the Adi and Käthe Dassler Memorial Foundation, Holdorf admitted that sometimes the athletes found Dassler's constant interventions irritating. 'We would say [of a pair of shoes], "Right, that's good now, it's fine", but he would keep at it, and we would always end up [conceding] that it was a good job he tested [his shoe designs] as long as he did. Somebody who could do absolutely anything [in sport] was a huge advantage for a sporting goods company. I think it's what gave him the drive to be the best, at least in his business. If he hadn't been a successful sportsman he wouldn't have been such a meticulous inventor.'

LEFT: Bobby Moore (left) playing for England and Uwe Seeler (right) playing for Germany at the 1966 World Cup.

That inventiveness paid well. By the end of the 1960s, Adi Dassler had been awarded the German Order of Merit, First Class, for his contribution to German business, and his company had opened a further 14 factories. It was making over eight million shoes a year. The patents registered by the company came thick and fast: for football boots with screw-in cleats; for track shoes with lightweight nylon soles, leather uppers and replaceable spikes; even for a rubberized moulded sandal that could be worn in the shower and which later proved an unexpected hit (see pages 89–93).

Small wonder then that in 1971 Joe Frazier and Muhammad Ali wore Adidas boots for what was dubbed the 'Fight of the Century', that the following year 80 per cent of gold medallists at the Munich Olympics wore Adidas shoes, and that Stan Smith won Wimbledon in them the same year. The following decade saw the company outfit a diverse range of world-class sportspeople – from the Argentine football squad to Romanian superstar gymnast Nadia Comăneci and the Italian mountaineer Reinhold Messner. Adi Dassler, or 'The Chef', as he was called within the company, had cooked up an impressive success story in around 25 years.

RIGHT: A poster promoting a Frazier-Ali fight, Frazier here wearing Adidas.

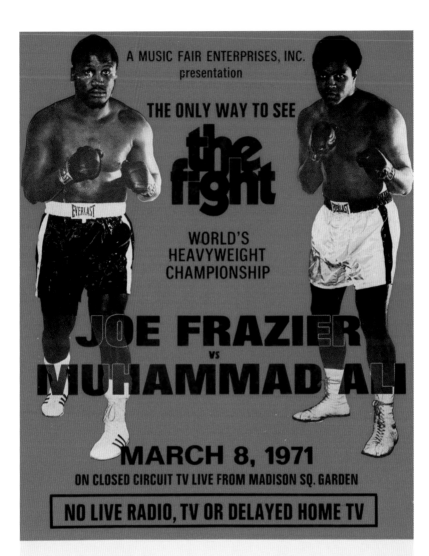

ALLENTOWN FAIR GROUNDS

Prices: $ 15.00, $ 12.50

Tickets on Sale NOW at the Allentown Fair Grounds

From Innovation to Style

Perhaps there was a gear-change in the company's approach to the aesthetics of its shoes too. In the 1960s and 1970s Adidas launched a number of styles that would come to be considered sneaker classics, still (after the occasional holiday) in production today: the likes of the Gazelle from 1966 (see pages 101–107), originally designed as a shoe for high jumpers and worn by Dick Fosbury, the athlete who perfected backwards jumping style known as the 'Fosbury Flop'; the Tournament (later renamed as the Campus) from 1970 (see pages 107–111); the shell-toed Superstar of hip-hop fame from 1969 (see pages 93–100); and the Nizza from 1975, Adidas's answer to the casualwear-friendly Converse Chuck Taylor. In clothing Adidas's visability grew through the creation, in 1972, of its Trefoil logo.

In the 1960s and 1970s Adidas launched a number of styles that would come to be considered sneaker classics.

Much of the later success of Adidas would not be witnessed by the family that laid the foundations: Adi Dassler died in 1978, the year he became the first non-American to be admitted to the National

LEFT: Romanian gymnast Nadia Comăneci wearing Adidas.

BELOW: Adolf Dassler with his many classic shoe designs.

Sporting Goods Industry Hall of Fame. He was buried at the opposite end of the cemetery from his brother. Käthe Dassler would die three years later, having expanded sales such that Adidas produced 102 million pairs of shoes a year and was now the world's biggest sporting goods manufacturer. Their son Horst, who took over the running of the

headquarters in Herzogenaurach, would die in 1987, aged just 51.

By the end of the 1980s Adidas was listed on the German stock exchange as Adidas AG Stock Corporation, and over the next three years all other members of the Dassler family gradually sold their majority shareholding, thus marking the end of an era. And the beginning of tricky times: without the strong leadership of its founding family, Adidas faced bankruptcy.

The company was rescued by the French businessman Bernard Tapie – controversial owner of cycling and football teams and, at one time, a French government minister – who in 1990 led a buy-out of Adidas for 1.6 billion francs and instigated a number of important reforms. He recruited Rob Strasser, the former head of design at a still fledgling US company by the name of Nike, modernized the Adidas logo (from the Trefoil to the three-striped triangle), moved most manufacturing to Asia and then listed the company on the stock exchange.

LEFT: The Gazelle.

Tapie's efforts started a process but didn't complete Adidas's recovery. In 1993 it came under the ownership and leadership of Robert Louis-Dreyfuss, an ex-pharmaceuticals and advertising industry businessman, who two years later took the company public. Over the next eight years, Louis-Dreyfuss helped build Adidas into a global name. (Notwithstanding his involvement in a scandalous attempt by a number of German officials to bribe FIFA execs to host the 2006 World Cup in Germany – investigated by FIFA in 2016 but later dropped owing to a statute of limitations expiring.) He did this, he conceded, changing as little about Adidas as possible, except perhaps upping the ante on marketing. As the advertising line explained simply: 'We knew then. We know now.'

'I suddenly realized . . . this guy Adi was the father of 90 per cent of the [sportswear] industry.'

Louis-Dreyfuss steered Adidas through a period of expansion. In 1997 it made its first acquisition, of the Salomon skiing brand. The following year it created its new headquarters, World of Sports, based around an old US military base that the company acquired in partnership with Adi Dassler's hometown of Herzogenaurach.

Although Adidas – under CEO Herbert Hainer – would sell Salomon just seven years later, in 2006 it would acquire Reebok, bringing together two historic sportswear brands that would, the same year, lead to the creation of the Adidas Group. Rockport, another, more outdoorsy footwear brand that had come under the Adidas umbrella, was also sold off in 2015, as was Reebok, in 2022. By that year, refocused once again around the Adidas name and under the leadership of CEO Kasper Rørsted, it was a US$22 billion-plus company, making 420 million pairs of shoes every year.

That made it the biggest sportswear company in Europe and, after Nike, the second largest in the world. But credit where credit is due. When Rob Strasser, the Nike marketing executive charged with destroying rival Adidas, was finally being wooed by the very same company, he was taken around the company museum. 'I suddenly realized that, with the exception of the waffle trainer and that air bag [Nike's Air Max technology], this guy Adi was the father of 90 per cent of the [sportswear] industry,' he would tell *Portland Monthly* in 2016.

And the world's third largest sportswear company? That was still Puma. Adi Dassler may have been pleased with that even from beyond the grave.

Adidas can claim to be among the biggest sporting goods companies in the world. But its appeal has come not just through innovation, but also presentation: from its Trefoil logo to its three stripes, its branding has attained a visibility and a credibility that has helped it endure both as a company and as a pillar of style culture for over a century.

The Three Stripes

If other sportswear companies focused their branding around the design and profile-building of a clear and impactful logo – famously Nike's Swoosh, for example – the Dassler story started out with something much less effective. Its busy ident was a shield, in which a large bird – an albatross perhaps – appeared to be struggling to carry a shoe.

When the Dassler brothers split, Rudolf Dassler seemed to appreciate the merit of a memorable logo for his new company, with Puma's leaping big cat in profile, but Adidas's first logo still left much to

RIGHT: Adidas advertising through the years.

Great athletes start here.

At adidas, we make shoes for some of the world's greatest athletes.

Now, with the same care and attention to detail, we make shoes for children.

They come in 12 styles, in lots of bright, fun colours and in sizes from 8 upwards. Pictured here, we have the Clipper, Tornado, Saturn and Scamp.

As you'd expect, they're built to last.

Which is really just as well when you consider what they might lead to.

adidas

WHAT DO YOU GET OUT OF A SHOE BASED ON THE FOOT?
WITH THE FEET YOU WEAR' EQUIPMENT ULTIMATE
YOU GET ROUNDED EDGES FOR BETTER STABILITY. YOU GET AIRPIECE IN THE HEEL
FOR SHOCK ABSORPTION AND YOU GET
A SHOE WITH
A LOWER PROFILE, LEAVING YOUR FEET CLOSER TO THE GROUND
ENABLING YOU TO

IMPROVE YOUR REACTION TIME

adidas The Big Name in Sports Footwear!

A 'ARGENTINIA' B 'VALENCIA' C 'CADET'

adidas *The mark of a winner*

Monday, back to work.

PERFORMANCE ESSENTIALS

adidas

next

FOREVER SPORT

be desired. Under the name 'Adolf Dassler' was the phrase 'Adidas Sportschuhe' and, in between, a spiked runner's shoe between two stripes extending from the Ds of the company name. There was one touch of more modernist thinking: Adidas was rendered in lowercase type, something the company has maintained as a corporate communications device ever since.

Zoom in on that first logo though and there was a great idea for a more graphically powerful alternative, hiding in plain sight: the three stripes, a design with which the company was fast becoming associated. Dassler had experimented with variations of anywhere between one and six parallel stripes, settling on three as the most graphically arresting: visible to stadium audiences at some distance, showing up well in photos and still easily sewn down the side of each shoe. A particularly successful football boot design – one that was made up of three parallel strips of leather, bringing more stability to the shoe – only seemed to cement the connection.

BELOW: The evolution of the Adidas logo.

1971

1991

But when Dassler had it in mind to put this logo on a more formal footing, he found that, unfortunately, another sportswear brand – the struggling Karhu, in Finland – already owned the idea as its trademark. Dassler's solution? In 1949 he bought it from Karhu, paying just a few hundred Deutschmarks and sweetening the deal with two bottles of whisky. And so, with a clink of glasses, Adidas, as the company was becoming known, became 'the brand with three stripes'.

These three stripes worked well when applied to shoes, but were less successful on the clothing that the company had started making in 1952; yes, they were boldly distinctive but, in a way, too obtrusive. The three stripes worked poorly in isolation too – on corporate documents, for instance. What was needed was something smaller and more versatile that was perfect for a shirt breast, like Lacoste's crocodile, an Admiral's naval cuff, or Wilson's big bold 'W', to cite some examples. With the Munich Olympics of 1972 returning the focus of one of the biggest events in sport to Germany, Adidas perhaps

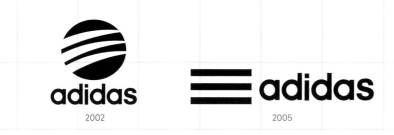

2002

2005

felt under pressure not to miss the opportunity
to make a splash.

It was at the event that the company unveiled its
Trefoil – a trident or leaf-like shape, into which could
be incorporated the three stripes for which Adidas
was already known. Each apex of the leaf was
thought to represent Adidas's now extensive reach
across the three continents of Europe, Asia and the
Americas. The Trefoil wasn't just unveiled either, but
tested: the Olympics was the first occasion on which
Adidas outfitted the German Olympic team, and
others, head-to-toe, though the Trefoil wasn't used
on footwear until 1976.

The 1972 Olympics would prove an effective
launchpad for Adidas as a lifestyle as much as a
sports brand, looking the part while reminding the
audience of its serious sporting credentials; among
other victories, the Soviet-Ukrainian sprinter Valeriy
Borzov won double gold in the 100m and 200m
wearing Adidas shoes. Inevitably though, such things
would be overshadowed by the murder at the
Olympics of eleven Israeli athletes by the Palestinian
militant organization Black September.

Nonetheless, the importance of a visual identity
clearly struck home. When, 15 years later, Adidas
felt it needed a fresh spark it hired Peter Moore
and Rob Strasser, ex design and marketing bigwigs
at Nike and now running their own sports

consultancy firm. They advised ditching the Trefoil for something even more direct: the three-bar 'mountain' logo, strictly used in just four colour options for Adidas's new Equipment line (later renamed Performance), a 'best of' Adidas collection they devised to emphasize the brand's heritage in making essential products.

'The model was to go back to what Dassler had tried to do all his life, which was to make the best products for the athlete to compete in,' Moore once explained. And, indeed, the refocusing on performance products helped rescue the brand from a slump and restore employee confidence. Performance products still account for around three-quarters of the company's sales.

Originals

Strasser and Moore also realized a means of doing what Adidas had long failed to achieve, which was to create a parallel life for the company as a lifestyle brand. Adidas was, after all, sitting on a goldmine of shoe styles that may no longer have been cutting-edge in terms of their materials or construction, but which had authenticity and historical resonance, and had a passionate following among various style tribes.

They also realized that effectively relaunching this family of shoes – upgraded in terms of fit, materials, comfort and quality – would require a new name,

and settled on 'Originals'. The Trefoil seemed
ideally suited to the shoes in this family and would
subsequently be used uniquely for them. Originals
was launched in 2001 – albeit a decade after Moore
and Strasser's initial proposal – and proved an
inspired example of brand-building, creating, in a
sense, an entirely new business out of designs that
Adidas already had. It underscored the brand's
pedigree, while at the same time shifting it into
the world of fashion. Styles like the Stan Smith,
launched in 1965, became a cult shoe once again,
decades later, selling tens of millions of pairs. 'Once
Innovative, Now Classic, Always Authentic', as the
advertising line had it.

It is perhaps ironic that Strasser would play such a
crucial part in Adidas's millennial revival. At Nike he
was legendary for his hatred of Adidas: it was he
who, when charged with wooing Wimbledon's
All England Lawn Tennis Club away from Adidas,
showed the club officials a large black-and-white
photo of Wimbledon's tennis courts after they had
been bombed by Germany during the Second
World War. His pointed tagline? 'Brought to you by
the people who wear three stripes' (as reported by
The Portland Monthly, 2016). It worked.

LEFT: Footballer David Beckham, basketballer
Kevin Garnett and rapper Estelle appear in the
2008 Adidas Originals ad campaign, 'House
Party', to celebrate '60 Years of Soles and Stripes'.

ABOVE: Hailey Baldwin wearing the Adidas Originals line in 2018.

Strasser and Moore would go on to establish Adidas America in Portland, Oregon – Nike's spiritual home. Moore would also briefly serve as Adidas's CEO, following Strasser's unexpected death aged just 46. Phil Knight, Nike's CEO, is said to have never forgiven Moore. 'It might have been okay if he'd just quit,' Knight once wrote. 'But he went to work for Adidas. An intolerable betrayal.'

Impossible is Nothing

Comparisons with Nike were always going to be impossible to avoid, as in any industry dominated by two giants. Now Adidas had both its advanced, sports-driven shoes, and clear water between those and its style-led ones – as Nike did between, say, its Flyknit and its Dunk. Perhaps all that Adidas still lacked was a reply to Nike's 'Just Do It' slogan. It had dabbled with slogans in its advertising before – 'Who's Coming Second?', 'Catch The Fever', 'More Power To You' – but none had stuck. Then, in 2004, came 'Impossible is Nothing'. The line was inspired by the boxer – and Adidas shoe-wearer – Muhammad Ali, who featured in the launch campaign alongside footballer David Beckham, long-distance runner Haile Gebrselassie and NBA star Tracy McGrady.

'Impossible is just a big word thrown around by small men who find it easier to live in the world they've been given than to explore the power they have to change it,' ran Adidas's new manifesto. 'Impossible is not a fact. It's an opinion. Impossible is not a declaration. It's a dare. Impossible is potential. Impossible is temporary. Impossible is nothing.'

That may well sound like something Ali would have said, in one of his typical bouts of philosophical boasting – and it has certainly often been mis-attributed to him subsequently. But it was, in fact, written by TBWA\Chiat\Day copywriters Boyd Coyner and Aimee Lehto Schewe. 'Impossible is Nothing' was sidelined a few years later in favour of 'Adidas Is All In', but was revived again in 2021 and arguably remains the sporting goods company's most effective slogan.

Sports brands would come to dominate street style in ways few of its global players could have anticipated, and in ways that few actually wanted. Specialists in all things sport, style was – officially at least – beyond their remit. Yet the story of Adidas shows how, like it or not, culture can embrace a brand, giving it resonance far beyond the stadium or track.

Run-DMC

It may be apocryphal, but it is said that Adidas had no idea about hip-hop stars Run-DMC's love affair with the brand – more specifically its Beckenbauer tracksuit, M45k BEST leather bomber jacket and, supposedly in imitation of prison-uniform style, unlaced Superstar shoes. That was until Adidas executive Angelo Anastasio was invited by Run-DMC's co-manager Lyor Cohen to one of their shows at Madison Square Garden in 1986. There, at the right moment, the band invited the audience members to hoist their Adidas items in the air. And there were, much to a dumbfounded Anastasio's amazement, a lot of them among the 40,000-strong audience. It was a sea of stripes.

RIGHT: Run-DMC wearing Adidas.

After all, while its products were available in the
United States, Adidas had only launched a US arm
for its business that year and was no doubt
wondering why sales had suddenly spiked. That
may have had something to do with the release by
Run-DMC of 'My Adidas', the first single from their
third album, *Raising Hell* (1986).

The song was written in response to a poem by
Gerald Deas, an activist who lived in the same
neighbourhood as Run-DMC, in which he drew
a connection between those who wore sneakers
(outside of sporting purposes) and criminality –
notably, drug dealing. Run-DMC wanted to put
that idea straight: to them sneakers were symbolic
of style, status and culture.

As group member Darryl 'DMC' McDaniels would
explain, the song grew out of the simple pleasure
they shared in 'wanting to talk about their sneakers
. . . More than just how many pairs they had.' It was
an attempt to express genuine appreciation for
a piece of design and – this being the early days
of hip-hop – move beyond the association of
sportswear-as-streetwear with troublemaking.

Whether or not Cohen was angling for some kind
of deal remains unclear. After all, Run-DMC hadn't
invented streetwear's affection for Adidas –
breakdancers had worn Superstar, Campus and
Gazelle shoes for their style and comfort for years,

much as skateboarders would also come to discover the same designs. One of the earliest specialist skateboard shoe brands, Etnies, was said to be making a sly nod to Adidas by tipping its E logo on its side to mimic its three-stripes branding.

What is clear is that, after his experience with Run-DMC, Anastasio called an emergency meeting with his fellow executives and argued that Adidas had to get behind this phenomenon. They, it's been said, were less than enamoured by the prospect but, all the same, found US$1 million for a sponsorship deal.

After all, the song, and Run-DMC's vocal and visual support of Adidas, had been the biggest free publicity promo any sportswear brand has been lucky enough to get, then or since: a publicity photo of the group wearing their fat gold rope chains over their Adidas Firebrand tracksuits, with Adidas Rivalry or Superstar sneakers and Kangol hats, would become a classic image of the era.

It was through the subsequent relationship with the group – the first ever official collaboration between the music and sportswear industries, paving the way for countless similar arrangements – that Adidas really got a foothold in the US, not to mention credibility as much in street culture as in sports. It was Run-DMC that popularized the idea of wearing Adidas sneakers more like a slipper, without laces, tongue proudly upright.

While the coming together of East Coast urban grit and German business precision may have been a serendipitous if unlikely pairing, Adidas could hardly have chosen a better act to team up with: Run-DMC would become the first hip-hop act to get a gold record, the first to have their videos played on MTV, the first to take the cover of *Rolling Stone* magazine and the first to win a Grammy nomination.

Casuals

Much as Adidas was co-opted by hip-hop in the US, so its shoes had, similarly, already been taken out of sportswear and put into fashion by style subcultures across Europe, especially in the UK. There, the Casual movement – a hugely influential British style movement growing not out of shared tastes in music, but out of the football fandom of the mid- to late-1970s – launched a trainer culture with Adidas at its core. Years before Moore and Strasser devised Adidas Originals, Casual helped to make classics out of certain models that otherwise might well have disappeared into back catalogues, among them the Stan Smith, Forest Hills, Harvard, Gazelle, Samba and Trimm Trabb, as well as States and Argentina from Puma.

RIGHT: Victoria Beckham wearing a pair of Stan Smiths.

Many of these came to the UK from Germany for the first time through Casual. There was cachet in wearing what could not be had at home, and access to these goods came through cheap travel to away matches on the European continent. But Casual also pioneered the idea of sportswear as fashion in the UK, appreciated for its relatively outlandish graphic content, colour and comfort.

'I believe [that Adidas] is intrinsic to culture,' as Gary Aspden, a long-time brand consultant to Adidas and curator of its Spezial line, put it to *Dazed* in 2013. 'When we [in the UK] were breaking into warehouses and doing acid-house parties in the late 1980s, we were all wearing the Adidas ZX Torsion range. You know, our shoes were really important to us. They were signifiers, a very subtle form of communication. When I was buying into Adidas as a youth we were buying our trainers from shops that sold tennis rackets, cricket bats and air rifles. We were actually taking something, adapting it and changing the context of it.'

In fact, Adidas's pop cultural resonance could be said to predate hip-hop, acid house and Casual. They may not have been wearing them as style statements as such, but Adidas shoes were favoured in the 1970s by the likes of, for example, Jim Morrison,

LEFT: Reggae star Bob Marley playing football wearing Adidas.

for some touch football. Bob Marley was a fan of Atlanta SPZL shoes and Copa Mundial boots, bright yellow Trefoil t-shirts and the Beckenbauer tracksuit (he wore one in a 1988 World Cup Adidas commercial). It's been said that Marley liked Adidas in part because the name sounds like Addis Ababa, the capital of Ethiopia and the birthplace of Rastafarianism. He could certainly claim to be one of the first stars to wear head-to-toe sportswear off as well as on the playing fields.

The Sex Pistols' Paul Cook and even David Bowie wore Adidas shoes, too. The latter preferred boxing boots, worn with a suit naturally, and Stan Smiths – a fact Adidas would pay homage to with the launch of a 'Ziggy' edition of the tennis shoe.

Nu-metal

Adidas's pop-cultural resonance did not stop with hip-hop and acid house either. Adidas would chime with nu-metal bands such as Limp Bizkit (an illustrated character prominently wears Superstars on the cover of their album *Significant Other*, 1999) and Korn (who had a subversive 1987 hit with 'A.D.I.D.A.S'). That may have been an acronym for 'All Day I Dream About Sex', an in-joke between the staff of the sports shop where frontman Jonathan Davis had once worked. But it was also a nod to the disruptive, more alternative-than-alternative aspect of a metal band of any kind wearing colourful German sneakers and shiny tracksuits, a style their

fanbase happily emulated. Not for nothing was their type of music dubbed 'Adidas rock' by some critics.

ABOVE: Nu-metal band Korn wearing Adidas.

'It was about breaking the mould,' as Davis would describe the band's Adidas-based style to *Kerrang* in 2021. 'It was about smashing down walls . . . and going against everything that metal was supposed to be.' A high-school DJ favouring old-school hip-hop, he was inevitably influenced by the style of Run-DMC. 'I just thought "that's a cool-ass look",' he has said. 'I could get down with that.' The eclectic style that their fanbase appreciated also made it hard for music industry executives to conveniently pigeonhole them. 'It was like, "What do we do with these f**kers?",' Davis recalled. 'This guy's playing bagpipes and wearing a f**kin' tracksuit!'

Like the executives, Adidas wasn't sure what to do with Korn either. It was willing to fit Korn out in some free merchandise, through stopped short of signing any sponsorship deal. 'Their reply was "Adidas is a sports company. We do sports, not music",' a disbelieving Davis has said. 'I would look out into the crowd and see all these kids wearing Adidas shit at our shows, but they couldn't do anything for us.' That decision came at a cost. Who stepped in with a US$500,000 sponsorship deal in 1998? Puma, of course, with Rudolf Dassler's company even putting the band in commercials to target nu-metal fans. 'We were just like, "F**k yeah! That's more than Adidas ever did for us!" It wasn't a sell-out thing. It was about respect,' explained Davis.

As Davis would also imply, maybe it was a matter of bad timing: Adidas had yet to properly understand its pop-cultural importance, let alone embrace it. And anything too left field was likely a trickier proposition for Adidas bigwigs.

Not that Adidas was short of yet more accidental, high-profile support. Over the following few years Jay Kay, frontman of Jamiroquai and ardent Adidas collector, was barely seen out of a pair of Gazelles – prominently so in the video for 'Video Insanity' (1996) – not to mention Adidas t-shirts and track

LEFT: Jay Kay from Jamiroquai performing in Adidas.

tops. Eventually he would get his own Oregon JK shoe. He'd even go online in 2023, noting that he had run out of the style and jokingly pleading to 'Dear Uncle Adidas . . . would you please make some more?' Uncle Adidas duly obliged. As Jonathan Davis would note, it wouldn't be long before the floodgates to lucrative collaborations opened: 'Then you've got Kanye West and all these other people with their own [custom Adidas] shoes . . .'

In the UK Britpop was spiced up by the press around a faux battle between supposed rival bands Blur and Oasis, but at least both of them could agree on their penchant for Adidas, with the Gazelle and Samba dominant. Blur would namecheck Adidas – their 1999 album *13* includes the song 'Trimm Trabb' – while the frontmen of both bands would go on to design their own shoes for Adidas's Spezial line.

Yeezy

It might seem that eventually Adidas got the message: music could be a medium for its products that it could actively encourage. And it did. The new century would see collaborations with Pharrell Williams, Beyoncé Knowles and Missy Elliott, who in 2004 launched a fashion line with Adidas under the name Respect M.E. 'I've been a fan of Adidas since Run-DMC,' Elliott said, inevitably.

RIGHT: Britpop star Noel Gallagher of Oasis performing in London in 1994.

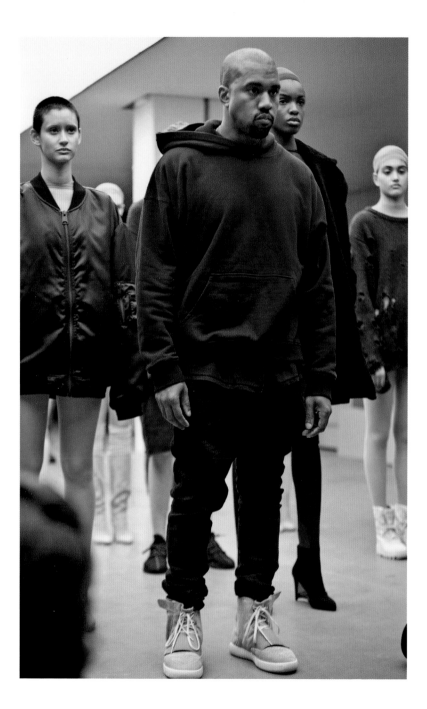

But it was perhaps Adidas's collaboration with Kanye West and his Yeezy brand – named after the 'Kanyeezy' nickname Jay-Z had given him and launched late 2013 – that drew the most attention, and not least because the rapper had been designing shoes for Nike. He'd made a very public exit from that company, complaining that it had failed to pay his due royalties. Much like one-time Nike executive Rob Strasser, West made what, in Nike's eyes, was the worst possible riposte and went over to the opposition. What followed was a testament to the importance of historic brands chiming with younger audiences, especially through a mix of celebrity association and more outlandish design. But it was also a demonstration of how hard such associations can be to manage.

Adidas signing with Kanye was a huge coup, not only because – relative to Nike at least – Adidas was in poor shape. In 2013 sales for Adidas in the US were falling, while Nike's were climbing. In one authoritative sneakerhead round-up of the best sneaker releases of the year, Adidas had just five shoes; Nike had 30. But just three years later – after the release of sneaker hits like the Yeezy Boost 750, with its zip-up heel, and the Yeezy 350 'Turtle Dove' in a flecked Primeknit – Adidas sales were almost up one-fifth, twice Nike's increase.

LEFT: Kanye West wearing Yeezy 750s at New York Fashion Week in 2015.

The then president of Adidas North America, Mark King, had no doubt about why: 'I think Kanye definitely helped make [Adidas] cool again,' adding that he thought it was also about a good working relationship. 'Had it only been Kanye, it would have gone up and gone down very quickly.'

In 2016 Adidas struck a new deal with West that would have seen him designing for the company for the decade to follow. Adidas called it the 'most significant partnership between a non-athlete and a sports brand'. The partnership seemed to prove inspirational to Adidas – its own shoe designs, the likes of the NMD or the Ultraboost, suggested a new, more modern approach. In 2019, Yeezy alone was making sales of over US$1 billion for Adidas, and a small fortune in royalties for West too.

RIGHT: Model Adut Akech in the Adidas x IVY PARK tracksuit, a collaboration with Beyoncé Knowles.

BELOW: Adidas x Pharrell Williams Solar HU NMD.

But then Adidas found itself slipping into a PR nightmare, unable to manage the chaotic comments

of someone who was, in a sense, still an outsider to the company, a free agent not tied to corporate expectations. West's opinions and his politics risked offending the Adidas audience. Adidas weathered the storm, feeling the need to justify its relationship with West, not least because Yeezy sales continued to grow and were expected to hit US$2 billion by the end of 2021.

West also became more demanding: he requested a seat on Adidas's board and said that he would wear Nike Jordans until he got it. Then he accused Adidas of ripping off his Yeezy slide design with a new version of its Adilette. 'This is for everyone who wants to express themselves but feels they can't cause they'd loose [sic] their contract or be called crazy,' he wrote. West made off-colour comments about the CEO Kasper Rørsted dying, and about his plans to end all his brand contracts, following that by terminating his deal with Gap.

Finally, in 2022, when Kanye West was alleged to have promoted anti-Semitic tropes about Jewish power on social media, Adidas was compelled to cut ties with the rapper, albeit somewhat late in the day and after the pressure of a social-media campaign against the company. Adidas's hesitation was understandable from the perspective of the bottom line: Yeezy was said to represent a full 10 per cent of the company's revenue. And it had some US$750 million of Yeezy inventory – which it would eventually decide to sell, donating a proportion of the profits to charity. Adidas would, at least, still hold the rights to as yet un-released Yeezy designs.

A *New York Times* investigation later revealed just how troubled the relationship between Adidas and Kanye West was from the start; West reportedly expressed his dislike of a proposed Yeezy shoe design by drawing a swastika over it, a symbol banned in Germany.

'The thing about me and Adidas is like, I can literally say anti-Semitic shit and they can't drop me,' West would say on a podcast. He was wrong.

Fashion

Music was not the only line of enquiry into pop culture that Adidas could follow. Of course, actively building relationships with sports stars was something that came naturally to Adidas, and it could count any number of icons among them, from tennis star Ilie Năstase to Formula One bad boy James Hunt, football giant Gerd Müller to basketball great Kareem Abdul-Jabbar.

Others, with the benefit of hindsight, it perplexingly let slip away. When, in the mid-1980s, basketball legend Michael Jordan was presented with a remarkable sponsorship deal to sign with Nike, he still wanted to be with Adidas. 'I went back to my Adidas contact and said, "This is the Nike contract –

if you come anywhere close I'll sign with you guys"', Jordan once recalled. Then, still too wrapped up in the merits of product over promotion, Adidas didn't get it. And didn't get Jordan.

As with sport, so Adidas's brand power ensured that it was a staple of TV and the cinema too. The huge 1970s cop show *Starsky & Hutch*, for example, saw Starsky wear a pair of SL72s week in, week out. Eddie Murphy wears a pair of Adidas Country in *Beverly Hills Cop* (1984) – prominently so on the poster. Sylvester Stallone and Michael J. Fox wear Adidas in *Rocky IV* (1985) and *Teen Wolf* (1985), respectively. Ewan McGregor wears a pair of Samba Supers in *Trainspotting* (1996), while Macaulay Culkin wears a pair of Adidas Forum in *Home Alone* (1990), an exact replica of which was reissued by Adidas in 2021, complete with burn marks, pertinent to the movie's plot. Adidas shoes, it seems, are even worn in the future: it's a custom pair of all-black Stan Smiths that Harrison Ford wears in *Blade Runner* (1982).

As with its relationship with sportspeople, this association with stars of both big and small screens was actively pursued by Adidas: in fact, a study of around 3,000 films and TV shows conducted in 2023 found that Adidas was the brand rated second

RIGHT: Eddie Murphy wearing Adidas Country in *Beverly Hills Cop* (1984).

He's been chased, thrown through a window, and arrested.
Eddie Murphy is a Detroit cop on vacation in Beverly Hills.

BEVERLY HILLS
Cop

PARAMOUNT PICTURES PRESENTS A DON SIMPSON/JERRY BRUCKHEIMER PRODUCTION IN ASSOCIATION WITH EDDIE MURPHY PRODUCTIONS·A MARTIN BREST FILM·
EDDIE MURPHY·BEVERLY HILLS COP·MUSIC BY HAROLD FALTERMEYER·SCREENPLAY BY DANIEL PETRIE, JR.·STORY BY DANILO BACH AND DANIEL PETRIE, JR·
PRODUCED BY DON SIMPSON AND JERRY BRUCKHEIMER·DIRECTED BY MARTIN BREST·MOTION PICTURE SOUNDTRACK ALBUM ON MCA RECORDS AND TAPES
A PARAMOUNT PICTURE

ABOVE: Michael J. Fox in *Teen Wolf* (1985).

highest for product placements, with 590; second only, again, to Nike. And yet Adidas's real pop-cultural power – which, arguably, trumped rivals Nike with gusto – was best expressed through its relationship with high fashion.

Indeed, while Adidas has made any number of tie-ins with important, if more niche, fashion brands and designers – A Bathing Ape, Craig Green, Fear of God, Palace, Moncler, Wales Bonner, and so on – it has also done so with several major league fashion names: Balenciaga, Raf Simons, Rick Owens, Gucci and Prada included. Stella McCartney and Yohji

Yamamoto would establish long-term working relationships with the sporting goods company.

ABOVE: Sylvester Stallone in *Rocky IV* (1985).

Such has been the longevity of Y-3 – the name given to the Yamamoto/Adidas collaboration when it was launched in 2003, taking the initial from 'Yamamoto' and the digit in reference to the 'three stripes' – that it would become well-established as a brand in its own right. Y-3 was known for: creating twists on established Adidas designs – draped tracksuit-style tops, for instance, two-tone Stan Smith shoes or the first 'designer' football strips and boots; extending its remit to new ones – for

ABOVE: Y-3 spring/
summer 2018
collection.

example, combat boots; and imagining the truly avant-garde – the likes of the Shibutsu boot.

That Y-3 survived so long was perhaps surprising, given how groundbreaking the project was initially – so much so, in fact, that when Yamamoto approached Nike first with the idea for a fashion/sport hybrid collection, 'their answer was very sharp and straight: "No, no, no. We will never make that. We are doing only sportswear",' as Yamamoto would recall. 'I made a call to Adidas and immediately they said yes.'

This led to the creation of an entirely new division for Adidas: Sports Style, alongside Performance and Originals. It also arguably opened the portal for a more direct relationship between high fashion and sportswear that many other companies would later capitalize on. As Yamamoto noted at the time of Y-3's launch, consumers were increasingly looking not to fashion designers for inspiration but to athletes and rock stars – one reason why he would later use the French football hero Zinedine Zidane to front his Y-3 collections. And yet it was very difficult to find sportswear that worked for everyday life: 'what I see now, the cut, the mix of colours, is awful', he said.

'We created something that did not exist before and completely projected into the future,' as Yamamoto would explain to *The Independent*. 'Y-3 opened a new . . . niche in the fashion and sportswear market. My desire was to make sportswear – in a sports and body-conscious age – elegant and chic. It's like a child born of two parents with an incredibly different DNA.'

That was an idea to run with: two years after the launch of Y-3, Adidas signed a deal with Stella McCartney to produce a sports-performance collection for women: everything from yoga pants to leggings, sports bras to gilets and running jackets. This was simply, if unimaginatively, called Stella McCartney by Adidas.

Aside from being ahead of the curve on the impending explosion in 'athleisure' style, McCartney's key contribution to Adidas was to push its products towards greater sustainability. In 2015, for example, Adidas's McCartney line included prototype shoes made from upcycled marine plastic waste – turned into a premium material by material science company Parley – that, within four years, saw the supply lines scaled up to allow for the production of over 11 million pairs.

McCartney also drove the Adidas Made To Be Remade circularity programme, using materials diverted from landfills, or the likes of Evrnu – an engineered fibre made from discarded clothing – that resulted in garments such as the Infinite Hoodie, designed to be both made from recycled materials and easily recyclable at the end of its life. She likewise partnered with Bolt Threads – another company specializing in bio-engineered sustainable materials – to create a tennis dress made from a cellulose-blended yarn and Microsilk, a proton-based material produced from sugar and yeast. Vegan Stan Smiths followed.

'I'd never want to sacrifice style for sport, [but] the reality is that when we started no one else was doing it [mixing fashion with performance sportswear] and no one knew where to sell it,' McCartney said of the collaboration in 2016. 'Now people understand it. And for us to keep ahead of it is through technology, which Adidas is at the forefront of.'

Of course these were mutually beneficial business relationships, Adidas providing the cult-like status of the sneaker world, high-end brands the allure of sophistication. Such was the enthusiasm of Adidas's move into this more upscale market that in 2023 it

RIGHT: Adidas Gucci autumn/winter 2022–23 collection.

took American fashion designer Thom Browne to court for using a four-bar stripe pattern on a variety of his shoe and activewear designs, arguing – unsuccessfully – that it was too easily confused with its three-stripe trademark. Jeremy Scott, another designer working with Adidas who's best known for his 'winged' and 'panda' hi-tops, would explain the deeper appeal of such collaborations.

'What I've always loved about Adidas is that they've always had a really organic connection to pop culture,' Scott said in *Complex* in 2011. 'It's been about music, fashion and inspiration and it's always been very genuine in that sense. When rave culture was about Adidas, they weren't freaked out about it, they said "Okay, cool!" They realized their vintage logo has another meaning to some people. When Run-DMC said they loved Adidas, they embraced it. [So many other brands] are kind of phobic of pop culture. [Meanwhile] I take [Adidas] some place that it hasn't been before, and that they're not doing internally.'

LEFT: Stella McCartney at the Adidas By Stella McCartney show, 2014.

Style

Adidas has a long story, but, from a design perspective, it also has two stories: that of what would come to be called Originals, and that of everything else. Many of the shoes that comprise Originals are museum pieces, from a technical standpoint. Yet it is precisely their simplicity, by 21st-century standards, that gives them their longevity, allowing them to touch many style cultures and also remain relevant, even as far more advanced products quickly come to look dated.

As dress codes become increasingly casual, in and out of the workplace, and when wearing sports shoes is more commonplace when not playing sport, Adidas has reaped the rewards: so many of its older styles, such as the Superstar and Stan Smith, look good with anything. Their inherent simplicity makes the Originals ideal for endless variations: tweak a colour or a texture and you have a whole new shoe. They have played their part in defining more than one generation's idea of comfort too.

RIGHT: Freddie Mercury of Queen wearing Adidas at Live Aid in 1985.

In more recent times, Adidas has successfully – arguably more so than its rival Nike – co-opted fashion to its cause. For every Originals fan, there is a customer for its loudest, most extreme, most extravagant designs – these qualities in many instances being a product of innovation. For every Adidas classicist, there is an Adidas avant-gardiste, for every minimalist, a maximalist.

Adidas's extended history, and its willingness to make shoes for more obscure sports, means its canon is vast. If only certain styles have become iconic, this is in no way indicative of Adidas's breadth of output. Frequent experimentation, while not always successful, has left many of its styles largely unknown. But it has left many more with acolytes just longing for a reissue. Inevitably then, so many styles can be given no more than a passing nod here.

To name a few not mentioned elsewhere in this book: Adicolor Hi (1984), packaged with markers so kids could customize them; ADAN (2001), the 'All Day All Night', a zip-up basketball shoe you were supposed to wear from court to nightclub; Edberg 86 (1986), the tennis player's signature shoe, helping to bring colour to the sport; Eldorado (1987), the best of Run-DMC's specials; Equipment Racing (1993), with its tongueless, sandal-like cut-out upper; the Spezial (1979), because even handball needed its own sneaker; Achill (1968), the

pioneering speed-laced running shoe; SL72 (1972), the multi-purpose training shoe and, arguably, the first cross-trainer; Forest Hills (1979), named after the neighbourhood in Queens, NYC, where the US Open was played up until the year before its release; Oregon (1982), a name that took a cheeky jab at Nike and the advent of Bill Dellinger's web shock-absorbency system; Top Ten (1979), better, perhaps, than the Air Jordan?

And these are just a few that could have been mentioned.

ABOVE: A 1998 ad for the Adidas Forum Supreme.

Samba

By the time of the 1950 World Cup, held for the first time in Brazil, Adidas had an established reputation as a maker of football boots. All the same, it wanted to benefit from the publicity around the event by creating a shoe that would mark the occasion: that shoe was the Samba. It would still be in production at the time of writing, despite its first incarnation being launched just four years after the end of Second World War. Indeed it is Adidas's second bestselling shoe after the Stan Smith, and, to date, its longest running (albeit over several variations).

There was much about the Samba, originally launched as a mid-top and more obviously a football-related shoe, that was innovative at the time: the 'sticky' brown gum sole had suction cups to give better grip on the hard or icy playing surfaces for which the Samba was designed; the upper was made from a thick black kangaroo leather; then, aesthetically, there was Adidas's trademark three stripes in white, and gold lettering. Accepting that the shoe was unlikely to find much immediate traction in Brazil, where frozen ground is a rarity, Adidas chose its name carefully – after the traditional Brazilian dance – to grab some headlines.

RIGHT: Model Gigi Hadid wearing a pair of Sambas.

ABOVE: The Samba in a traditional black and white colourway.

Such a specialist shoe was, perhaps expectedly, more of a hit with pro footballers across chillier Europe. But by the 1970s the Samba would find renewed life in football circles, both as the go-to shoe to wear for five-a-side on hardwood, concrete and artificial grass surfaces, but also among football fans, as the UK's Casual style subculture (see pages 48–52) adopted a more streamlined, lighter, low-cut version. This was not dissimilar to the Gazelle, but distinctive for the addition of a T-shape toe box and its combination of leather and suede.

ABOVE: Grace Wales Bonner x Adidas.

That diehard football fan Bob Marley would often be photographed wearing a pair of Sambas throughout the 1970s maybe helped spark interest beyond the sport. Certainly, the Samba couldn't be contained by football – it would be one of the first shoes to cross over into other sports by being embraced at the grassroots level. By the 1980s the benefits of the shoe, notably grip, stability and toughness, were appealing to skateboarders too, inspiring the creation and the look of Adidas's Busenitz skate shoe in 2006.

ABOVE: The Samba Primeknit.

By the 2010s, the Samba was discovered by celebrities and given new life through collaborations with fans including actor Jonah Hill, singer Beyoncé and designers including Fear of God, Craig Green and Grace Wales Bonner, whose influential interpretations arguably rebooted the Samba brand yet again. Adidas produced a special edition with British shoemaker Clarks too. Versions in bright colours – not the black and white that had signalled Samba for several decades – were introduced for the first time.

Not that the Samba left sport behind altogether: in 2014 Adidas launched the world's first football boot with a knitted upper, and considered it so revolutionary that a nod back through history seemed apt. It was named the Samba Primeknit. And in 2021 Adidas launched the Velosamba, a Samba with a window cut into the sole to accommodate two cleats of Shimano bicycle pedals.

Was this all part of Adidas CEO Bjørn Gulden's intention to capitalize on the Samba being what, in 2022, he called 'the hottest shoe on the market' by selling 'millions and millions' of pairs? Certainly, sales of Sambas had, reportedly, increased ten-fold over just twelve months. But the following year, after several summers in which the Samba repeatedly found itself to be the 'it' shoe, *GQ* magazine was asking, 'Have we over-hyped the Adidas Samba?' Such was fashion's way with Adidas shoes – when a style from its back catalogue was rediscovered, invariably it would become a trend phenomenon.

Stan Smith

The Stan Smith shoe is one of the most loved and bestselling sports shoes of all time. In 1988 the style made it into the *Guinness Book of World Records* for having sold in excess of 22 million pairs. At the time of writing, over 100 million pairs had been sold.

The shoe takes its name from the American tennis champion Stanley Roger Smith. When it was launched in 1963, the then French-made shoe was the signature product worn by French player Robert Haillet, and was known as the 'Haillet'. It wasn't all that dissimilar to other Adidas tennis shoes of the era: the Monte Carlo, Rod Laver or John Newcombe, for example.

That the shoe was a very simple, round-toed, decoratively minimal model in large part explained its early adoption as a style worn off court, with John Lennon and later David Bowie wearing them. Yet it was technically original for its time. It came in leather rather than the more typical canvas – an idea attributed to Adi's son and then Adidas CEO Horst Dassler – which improved durability and comfort, but also wasn't discoloured by sweat, a genuine issue when tennis players were expected to wear all white. Its perforated sides improved ventilation. These perforations took the form of three parallel lines, and the Haillet/Stan Smith is the only classic Adidas to nod towards the brand's trademark three stripes rather than actually having them.

Adidas, it seems, knew it had a classic shoe on its hands, and when Haillet retired in 1971, the company began to look for another player to take on the shoe as their own. In 1972 sports agent Donald Bell – who would later mastermind one of Michael Jordan's contracts with Nike – suggested Smith as an obvious candidate to Horst Dassler. Smith was, after all, now Wimbledon champion two years running and the new US Open champion too. Smith would be ideal for Adidas's push into the US market.

At Horst Dassler's suggestion Dassler, Bell and Smith met, much to Smith's surprise, at midnight in a Parisian nightclub to discuss the arrangement. '[We] watched all these women parading around in very elegant tuxedos,' Smith would recall. 'We were talking about a shoe deal, but I was having a hard time paying attention.'

ABOVE: The Stan Smith in its original green and white colourway.

The first shoes with 'Stan Smith' on them would come off the production line in 1973. However, his was not the only name. Confusingly, the shoe was known as the 'Stan Smith–Haillet' for the next five years, featuring the name of both players on the tongue, alongside a portrait of Smith. Some might not even have recognized that as being Smith, as the portrait was made during the only six-month period in his life when he didn't have a moustache. (Only a special skateboarding edition of the shoe from the 2000s updated the image to include what would become something of a bushy style signature for the player.)

'I remember returning serve, looking down at my shoes and seeing my own face there for the first time, which was a strange experience,' Smith would recall in the documentary *Who is Stan Smith?* (2022). '[And] a little later on I got upset because I lost to a guy who was wearing my shoes, which I didn't think was appropriate.'

When, on another occasion, Smith noticed that his opponent, also wearing his eponymous shoe, had crossed Smith's name out on his pair, Smith jokingly suggested to him that he couldn't like him much. The player told him that he was sponsored by another brand and shouldn't have been wearing Stan Smiths at all – but he preferred them.

'Some people think I am a shoe.'

From 1978 only Smith's name appeared on the shoe, though by now the model's appeal to tennis players was beginning to wane as more technically advanced products became available. But the Stan Smith shoe would begin its new life as a fashion accessory. Adidas had spotted this potential: although a staple of its Originals line-up, in 2011 the company stopped production of the Stan Smith

LEFT: Stan Smith playing at Wimbledon in 1972, wearing his eponymous shoe.

ABOVE: The simplicity of the Stan Smith makes it an ideal base for variations.

for two years (the resulting scarcity only serving to fuel hype about the shoe), relaunching a subtly updated version in 2013 for the Stan Smith-branded model's fortieth anniversary.

The Stan Smith would prove to be both a celebrity and fashion-shoot favourite. Yet it was a series of collaborations – with, for example, Pharrell Williams, Raf Simons and Stella McCartney – that helped boost interest. In a nod to the distinctive green heel tab and tongue graphic of the definitive 'cloud white' version of the shoe – and still the bestseller – even *The Muppets'* Kermit the Frog got an edition. The simplicity of the shoe invited easy customization and endless permutations: bold colours and two-tone versions; ones that experimented with vegan and other sustainable materials or were given a 'luxe' make-over; tie-ins with *Toy Story* or *Star Wars*; editions that swapped out the Stan Smith tongue portrait for celebrities such as Ellen DeGeneres; others that came with technical updates like Adidas's Primeknit or Boost.

Variations of the Stan Smith shoe were so abundant that, in the public consciousness, they would eclipse the sporting successes of the man whose name was given to them: 'The shoe is made by Adidas but it's part and parcel of me. Some people think I am a shoe,' Smith would quip to *Hypebeast* in 2022. 'A lot of people know me because of the shoe instead of my tennis career. [When it took off as a fashion shoe] it was definitely a shock to me at first. I viewed it as my "work shoe" when I was playing, so I didn't really think about people wearing it off the court.'

Not that he was complaining. If he didn't get his own signature shoe, and had to make do with another player's cast-off, Smith nonetheless received a royalty for every Stan Smith shoe sold. He has noted, though, that he is still not allowed to wear a pair of Stan Smiths in the Royal Box at Wimbledon.

Adilette Slides

That Adidas should, in the 2020s, find itself with another cult product, but this time in the form of a beach slider, would no doubt be amusing to Adi Dassler, a man who prided himself on developing highly technical products for specialist sporting use. However, in one way, the Adilette Slides fulfilled this brief.

Back in 1963 a football manager friend is said to have mentioned his specific problem to Dassler: that his players stepping into the communal showers after a match was like stepping into a pool of germs. Dassler immediately knew what the solution was: a simple, foam-injected, step-in shoe that, since it was waterproof, could be worn in the shower, with suction pads built into the soles (as they had been with his Samba shoes) to ensure plenty of grip in the wet.

He knew this because he had pondered the problem himself years before, making a prototype of sorts that he had worn around the garden on his days off. These had a wide sole and a wide band to hold the foot gently in place. It was a simple and elegant solution for crossing the garden back to the house.

But Dassler also knew that the technology wasn't yet mature enough to make such a product, at least not something this flexible. That all changed in 1970, when Dassler found the machine that could inject foam as he imagined. After two years of

RIGHT: The Adilette Slide.

experimentation, Adilette Slides – branded with three bold stripes over the vamp – were launched just before the 1972 Munich Summer Olympics. Swimmers at the event all took to the slides immediately, wearing them from changing rooms to poolside, as did many other athletes behind the scenes.

Yet Dassler soon identified a problem with the design. By 1975 he noted that the general sizing of the slides meant that they were not as comfortable as they could be for a broad variety of feet, and this was damaging sales.

'A major reason is that we cannot make the instep band adjustable because of the three stripes [over the vamp],' Dassler noted, according to papers held by the Adi and Käthe Dassler Memorial Foundation. 'This has proven quite a disadvantage because every foot has a different width and height. With the earlier model, footballers with high insteps could override the problem by not sliding their foot in and allowing their heel to protrude slightly over the back edge. However, our new moulded sole has such a high edge that [that is] no longer possible.'

Then there was the question of perception. It was a testament to the fact that customers had started to wear the Adilette not for its intended purpose, but as an everyday sandal, that complaints came in about how loose fitting they were. Dassler explained that 'from a medical and orthopaedic point of view' this was actually a benefit, since 'the foot is forced to work while walking, [thus] strengthening the muscles.' It was, he noted, the same principle as was applied to the 'health sandals' – the likes of Birkenstock – that were popular at the time.

Perhaps another solution would be to wear these 'shower shoes' over socks, as fashion followers would do in the 2010s. Mark Zuckerberg might have helped make them part of Silicon Valley's 'normcore' uniform, but then brands such as Celine and Chloé introduced luxury versions, prompting another boom in sales for the Adilette. Kanye West's Yeezy label would introduce his own beefier take on the slides while he was under contract to Adidas, though this did not stop him calling out Adidas in 2022 for making what he called a 'fake Yeezy' with its Adilette 22, actually just the latest version of the shoe it had invented.

Superstar

When the Superstar was launched in 1969, it was with no easy task in mind. The Converse Chuck Taylor shoe had dominated basketball since the

LEFT: The Superstar.

1920s, offering players next to nothing in the way of technological advances since then. But it was an American institution. Germany – when Adidas was very much viewed as a German or, at best, a European company – had no pedigree in basketball. And yet here it was with a shoe that was made from leather, when canvas was dominant in the sport, and was a low-top too. Then Adidas had the nerve to call it the Superstar.

In time the basketball world would come to see all of these qualities as advantages, not least as the sport became more athletic, and more aggressive, driven by players who had come up from streetball rather than the collegiate recruitment circuit. Besides, Adidas had nowhere else to go: by the mid-1960s it dominated track and field events, but to crack the US market it had to crack basketball.

It did so in spectacular fashion. Shoes like Adidas's Pro Model hi-top and 1965's Supergrip were being worn by leading players in the NBA towards the end of the decade. By 1973 some three-quarters of NBA players were estimated to be wearing Adidas. And three years later it signed a sponsorship deal with Kareem Abdul-Jabbar, then the NBA's star player. A decade later, basketball all-time-great Michael Jordan would famously really want to sign a

RIGHT: Kareem Abdul-Jabbar, left, playing in Superstars.

ABOVE: Rapper Missy Elliott wearing Superstars.

sponsorship deal with Adidas, not Nike. Adidas, almost equally famously, couldn't see the way to giving Jordan the deal he wanted.

But getting to this point would take the transformative design of the Superstar. The origins of the shoe – sometimes affectionately called the 'shell toe', after its clam-shaped toecap – lay in another Adidas basketball shoe, the Olympiade, created for the 1964 Tokyo Olympics. This Superstar took the Olympiade as its template, and upgraded it specifically to counter all of the new acute stresses of playing basketball: the padded tongue prevented tight lacing from limiting circulation; a wedge built into the heel stopped the shoe from crumpling on impact after a jump; it had an oversized heel counter to prevent the foot moving around inside the shoe, thus protecting the ankle; and it had a distinctive herringbone-pattern rubber sole for maximum grip. And then there was the feature for which it would become best known: the ribbed shell toe, an idea borrowed from Adidas's tennis model.

The result may have looked odd, relative to the norms of basketball shoes at that time, so Adidas went to source. Adidas consultant Chris Severn, who is credited with spotting the gap in the market that the old-fashioned Converse boot opened up, took pairs of Superstars to basketball courts around the US and convinced players to give the new shoe a go. 'They had played in canvas shoes all their life,' Severn notes in the book *Sneaker Wars* (2008). 'The Superstar shoe looked totally alien to them. [But] they weren't paid by Converse [to wear its shoes]. It was just habit.'

Experience quickly revealed the superiority of the Superstar as a secure, flexible, protective, agile shoe – qualities that also made it perfect for breakdancing, the urban dance form of the 1970s and 1980s that sat alongside the equally urban sport of streetball. As hip-hop became the defining urban music, one band in particular, Run-DMC, brought all of these strands together.

They did not look to stand apart in their dress, as more glamour-minded rock musicians had done before, but to embrace the style of the streets from whence they had come by wearing Adidas Beckenbauer tracksuits and Superstars. That Superstars were, at this time, still hard to come by only added to their kudos, with the group wearing them unlaced. It made them worth singing about too, as Run-DMC did with 'My Adidas', the 1986 song that led to a pioneering sponsorship deal (see pages 44–48).

By the 1990s, skateboarders would embrace the shoe too. But it was Adidas's collaboration in 2003 with Nigo, the designer behind cult Japanese streetwear label A Bathing Ape, that tipped the Superstar – or the Super Ape Star, as the spin-off was called – into high-fashion territory. Adidas did

not want to lose that momentum. In 2005 Adidas
followed the Super Ape Star with a series of 35
designs to mark the Superstar's 35th anniversary,
with collaborators including the diverse likes of Andy
Warhol, Disney and Missy Elliott. Lucky retailers saw
queues around the block.

The floodgates for Superstar fandom were open.
When, in 2015, Pharrell Williams collaborated on the

ABOVE: The Superstar
was ideal for
breakdancing.

Superstar 'Supercolor' project, Adidas released 50 different shades of the Superstar simultaneously – one of the biggest collaboration releases in sneaker history. Some people, it's said, bought every colour.

BELOW: The Superstar 'Supercolor' project.

Gazelle

In some respects, the Gazelle is an oddity in the canon of great Adidas shoes. It was built around a track shoe, for example, yet Adidas tested the shoe with both the West German football and handball teams. Indeed, appealing to all three sports for different reasons, the Gazelle was Adidas's first general-purpose sports shoe. One advertisement featuring the Gazelle would show it alongside images of sprinters, basketball players, tennis players and even American footballers. As the text put it: 'When your leisure time is spent on the go, you need equipment that just doesn't stop.'

The Gazelle was launched in 1966 and named at a time when Adidas was christening many of its shoes after wild animals, the Jaguar and Panther included. It was the first Adidas shoe to come in suede (more specifically kangaroo suede), at a time when most sports shoes were in less supple and heavier leather. Two years later, arch-rival Puma would release its first 'lifestyle' shoe in suede, the Crack – by turns renamed the Clyde and the Suede.

On its release, the Gazelle came in just two colours, red or blue, with Adidas's three stripes in white. The use of suede allowed those colours to be unusually vibrant relative to leather sports shoes. But this wasn't just an aesthetic choice: the red pair – Gazelle Rot ('red' in German) – came on a gum rubber, non-slip sole taken from the company's

ABOVE: The Gazelle Rot is ideal for outdoor use.

Olympiade shoe, cut with a waveform groove pattern that made it ideal for outdoor use. Mick Jagger and a young Michael Jackson would sport Gazelles in red.

In contrast, the blue pair – Gazelle Blau – had indoor use more in mind. It came on a ripple sole (borrowed from Adidas's 1960 Rom model) incorporating a microcell technology; this embedded tiny air bubbles into the rubber to provide greater cushioning. It was an idea that the sports footwear industry – including Nike – would run with. Adidas would continue to tweak the design over subsequent years, adding a heel tab to protect the Achilles tendon and a vinyl tongue that moulded around the foot. In 1972 it introduced a version with a hexagonal, polyurethane foam, microcell sole.

That was the year an American swimmer took the idea of pleasing his sports shoe sponsor to new heights. Encouraged by Horst Dassler not to let his track pants hide his blue Gazelles too much when he

stood on the podium to collect one of the staggering seven gold medals he won at the Munich Olympics that year, Mark Spitz took his shoe off and waved it in the air. Then he did it again after the US national anthem was played. The International Olympic Committee was not pleased with this flagrant product placement.

ABOVE: The Gazelle Blau is designed for indoor use.

As for more variation in the look of the shoe, that would not come until 1984, when the cultish Gazelle Grün, in lime green, was released, ahead of a plethora of colours being launched throughout the 1990s. It was in this decade that the Gazelle – as with so many Adidas shoes – made the transition from sports to fashion, as its general-purpose design perhaps suggested was the intention all along. The supermodel Helena Christensen posed nude except for a pair of Gazelles, while Kate Moss would be a flag-bearer for the style too. In the UK specifically, the Gazelle was the definitive sports shoe of the Britpop era, sported by those other arch-rivals, Blur and Oasis.

ABOVE: Liam Gallagher leaving Abbey Road Studios.

'When I gave up drugs I had to obsess about something, and I'm not into cars, not into jewellery and all that kind of thing, and I had loads of guitars, so I set off on a quest to collect Adidas trainers,' as Noel Gallagher would tell *The Independent* in 2013. Noel would get his own special edition of the Gazelle (and brother Liam an edition of the SPZL).

The stripped-back style of the Gazelle would also make it an ideal template in the age of sneaker-design collaborations with the likes of Japanese streetwear label Neighborhood, skate label Palace and even Transport for London (the authority charged with running the city's transport infrastructure). 'The silhouette is appealing to

ABOVE: The Gazelle.

so many groups because of its simplicity,' as just one of those collaborators, Brendon Babenzien, designer for menswear brand NOAH, would note in 2020. 'The [design of] Gazelles allows people to wear them in any number of ways and they take on the personality of the wearer. They are limitless.'

The Gazelle would certainly prove an invaluable template for Adidas. As Adidas brand consultant Gary Aspden would explain, 'the profile [of the Gazelle], the "T" toe overlay and the contrast of the white stripes against brightly coloured suede laid the foundations for so many shoes in the years that followed.' Even so, few might have imagined that the Gazelle would, in 2022, get an upgrade courtesy of Italian luxury fashion giant Gucci – first unveiled on the feet of Harry Styles – with their uppers and even rubber sidewalls shot through with Gucci's double-G logo.

Campus

The Gazelle, launched in 1966, encouraged Adidas to explore other shoe designs also using suede. In 1970 came the Greenstar, a training shoe first used by the Boston Celtics basketball team, in part because it came in a green that matched the team's uniform, and which inspired a number of other NBA teams to call for a shoe in their colours too.

LEFT: Harry Styles wearing Adidas x Gucci Gazelles.

Indeed, the Greenstar would be relaunched in the early 1970s as the Tournament, available in multiple hues of suede. This durable shoe – featuring 'lightness, comfort and top performance', as one advertisement read at the time – became a basketball staple, especially among college players. But the basketball world moved on, both stylistically and technologically, and, later that decade, the Tournament was shelved. However, foreshadowing the idea behind Adidas Originals by some 20 years, in 1980 Adidas concluded that while the Tournament no longer worked as a performance shoe, it did as a lifestyle model. That year the Tournament was relaunched, this time under the Campus name.

Adidas might well have hoped that the simple, accessible shoe would catch on with college students, as the shoe's name suggested. In the UK the Casual style movement certainly embraced it, but in the US the Campus remained in the

ABOVE: The Campus.

LEFT: The Beastie Boys wearing Adidas.

background, just one of a number of street-style options alongside the Gazelle and the Samba.

But, as with the Superstar, hip-hop group Run-DMC had a part in the Campus's street-style uptake; with the Superstar only being available in white at the time, Run-DMC turned to the Campus for some colour creativity. Then, in 1992, the Beastie Boys gave it their nod of approval too, with Mike Diamond wearing the style on the cover of their third album, *Check Your Head*. Diamond would subsequently launch his own X-Large streetwear label and New York store. One of its main draws? Its supply of rare, deadstock Adidas shoes.

The easy-going, fuss-free, wearable Campus was suddenly in the spotlight. In the UK Britpop took on the Campus as it had other classic Adidas styles. The shoe would subsequently undergo any number of variations, mostly featuring twists on colour and fabrication, making the Campus one of the more fun Adidas options.

In 2009 hip-hop group House of Pain, for example, collaborated on a pair in emerald green in tribute to its Irish roots; there was a black-and-white two-tone version, another Beastie Boys favourite; in 2011 a *Star Wars* collaboration came in a light grey fur finish and was signed Wampa, after the Yeti-like creature that almost kills Luke Skywalker in *The Empire Strikes Back* (1980); while in 2021 a *South Park* edition was made up in lilac towelling, the tongue logo replaced by a pair of eyes that looked bloodshot under ultraviolet lighting. In 2023 came the 'Croptober' model, taking its name from the annual harvesting of cannabis plants, typically every October. The style came wrapped in light brown paper, akin to rolling paper, that could be torn away as the wearer preferred to reveal a hairy green suede below, mimicking the colour of cannabis leaves.

NMD

If the relationship between Adidas and Puma was fractious – the two companies would eventually call a truce in 2009 by playing a symbolic football match in which the two teams were a mix of employees from both – then that paled into insignificance next to the rivalry Adidas would have with Nike. Playing catch-up with the American giant, and with its Jordan brand, Adidas knew that while its Originals business was hugely lucrative, and gave its brand the cachet of heritage, it also had to produce more progressive, contemporary designs too.

Nike was aware of the threat this posed. When, in 2014, Adidas poached three of its designers – Denis Dekovic, Mark Miner and Marc Dolce – to establish an Adidas design studio in Brooklyn, New York, Nike sued them for US$10 million, claiming that they had taken trade secrets with them (the case would be resolved in a confidential settlement). Signing with Kanye West – once he had left Nike too – was also a

ABOVE: The NMD.

step Adidas took towards exploring bold new ideas, rather than looking backwards into history. West's Yeezy sub-brand gave Adidas a share of the huge resale/aftermarket too, long overwhelmingly dominated by Nike and Jordan brands.

So, a lot was riding on the launch of the NMD (for 'Nomad') in 2015, a shoe that Nic Galway, Adidas's vice president of global design, told *GQ* was a way of 'connecting the past and the future in the most comfortable way . . . [The NMD] isn't just [about] how the product looks but how we live our lives. We all travel so much these days. The items you take have to have more meaning, culturally, and they also have to feel good.' He added that it was important for Adidas to 'always reference our history, and how it has affected culture', but conceded that 'if you stay stuck there it can become a limiting thing.'

GQ proposed that the NMD_R1 – the first of the NMD shoes – might well be 'the best Adidas sneaker of all time'. The NMD was certainly a 'best of' package in one shoe: with those 1980s-style colour-blocked panels on the midsole it harked back to the likes of Adidas's Boston Super, Rising Star and Micropacer models, but had a hi-tech Boost sole and a Primeknit upper. Certainly, it struck a chord: to secure a pair of NMDs people camped out overnight in some places and caused a life-threatening stampede in others. Almost immediately pairs went onto the resale market for five times the retail price – and sold.

'[The NMD] isn't just [about] how the product looks but how we live our lives.'

Many interpretations followed. There was a Chukka boot version and a City Sock one, a version with toggles, with 'cage-assisted' lacing, and one with no laces at all. And there were many collaborations, among them with Pharrell Williams' Humanrace (Hu) brand from 2016, with the luggage company RIMOWA, with White Mountaineering and with A Bathing Ape, all of which only served to fuel the NMD hype.

Some would suggest that the NMD was instrumental in Adidas becoming the second biggest footwear brand in the US in 2017, when it finally overtook Jordan, if not Nike. Others would suggest that the success of the NMD caused Adidas to oversaturate the market and delay in pursuing more new ideas. Later versions, such as the NMD S1 (for 'Sneaker 1') were applauded but couldn't reach the dizzy heights of the NMD's initial impact. All the same, several NMD revivals will almost certainly play a part in Adidas's future story.

Beckenbauer Tracksuit

If sportswear companies typically find their reputation grounded in the innovation and design of sports footwear, the all-important piece of equipment for athletes of all kinds, Adidas also found itself the owner of an icon in clothing too: the Beckenbauer tracksuit. Named after the all-time-great German footballer Franz 'The Kaiser' Beckenbauer, who was signed by Adidas in 1967 to wear it, this was a tracksuit most readily identified by the Adidas three stripes that ran along the outer seams of both sleeves and legs.

Of course, the idea of the tracksuit was not new, as athletes had been wearing a warm, two-piece all-cotton suit for training since the 1920s. What Adidas introduced was a suit made of what, in the 1960s, were still considered to be futuristic synthetic fibres. Consequently, the Beckenbauer was both lightweight and quick drying, but also had a distinctive sheen to it. The timing for this product

RIGHT: The Spice Girls' Melanie Chisholm wearing a Beckenbauer tracksuit.

could hardly have been better either; thanks in part to the efforts of rival sportswear manufacturer Nike, the early 1970s saw the healthy leisure pursuit of jogging take off in the US. Less cumbersome than traditional sweatshirt tracksuits, the Beckenbauer would prove ideal.

Yet it would be in pop culture that the tracksuit would really make an impact, for its visual appeal but also for its comfort – prefiguring the rise of athleisure and the dominance in street fashion of sweatshirts and pants. Through Bob Marley and Jamaican reggae in the 1970s, on to the breakdancing B-Boys of New York and to the Casuals subculture of the UK during the late 1970s and early 1980s, the Beckenbauer has been a remarkably recurrent style staple. Run-DMC, of course, made it their own, and made it an international fashion statement.

But not entirely their own. During the 1990s hardcore high-tempo ravers wore the tracksuit as part of Gabber, the Rotterdam, Netherlands-born style tribe that influenced an entire collection by Raf Simons and Gosha Rubchinskiy for Adidas in 2018. The Beckenbauer was a key element of the Tokyo-based Harajuku street style of the 1990s too – captured by photographer Shoichi Aoki on Omotesandō Avenue and its environs – and, back in the UK again, for Britpop. The tracksuit would resonate into the 21st century as well: with nu-metal in the US, with

Stormzy and the UK's Grime scene, and with fashion interpretations by Palace and Balenciaga.

While most sporting-goods companies create footwear classics, very few pull off the same trick in clothing: the exceptions – the Lacoste or Fred Perry polo shirt, for example – prove the rule. And yet every generation seems to find a way to make this Adidas tracksuit their own.

ZX Line

The fact that not all runners are the same was an important distinction that – led by designers Jacques Chassaing and Markus Thaler – birthed the ZX line of Adidas shoes, launching in 1984 with the ZX 500 and named with a nod to the Kawasaki ZX500 motorbike of the time. The ZX design thinking recognized that in order to maximize performance, running shoes had to be structured around the athlete – those who need more or less support, those who lean into their running action, and so on.

It would be through the ZX line that Adidas would launch the likes of its Soft Cell cushioning and Torsion stability technologies. The comfort, not to mention the distinctive colour choices, perhaps helped to make the model the shoe of choice among British acid house ravers during what was dubbed the 'second summer of love' in 1988 and 1989, or on Berlin's techno scene at the same time. 'The ZX lineage has enjoyed its longevity because from the beginning it was about designing something unique, something relevant, and something which met the needs of its consumers,' as Chassaing would explain in an interview with the sneaker retailer Footpatrol.

Indeed, the ZX line would prove successful precisely for bridging the gap between performance and lifestyle at a time when these two worlds were some way apart: running shoes were made stylish. Multiple ZX shoes would follow, each colour coded according to their particular emphasis on cushioning or support, guidance or racing, and each given a numeric designation – the three-digit 'hundred' series followed by the more technically advanced four-digit 'thousand' series.

'When you bring out something innovative and want to be successful, you need to make an impact; this can be done with the technology itself, but it can also be done aesthetically, with colour. With the thousand series the decision was to go with bright, aggressive colours,' Chassaing explained. 'But we wanted to stand out, even from the hundred series.'

Eventually, in 2019, came a five-digit product, the ZX 10000. As Adidas's Gary Aspden puts: 'The ZX prefix is sacrosanct for Adidas fans, so to try to tackle doing any new numbers in the ZX series should really be approached with caution and done respectively.

RIGHT: Rita Ora wearing the ZX 750.

[It's] the footwear equivalent of making a new *Star Wars* film.'

In 2008 Adidas launched the A-ZX line, inviting some 22 partners – from the Parisian store Colette to San Francisco's HUF – to interpret the ZX in their own way, arguably breaking ground on the whole idea of designer collaborations like those with Pharrell Williams and Kanye West.

In 2020 a Joshua Tree-themed ZX 5000 was released in collaboration with a less obviously fashionable partner, the US's National Park Foundation. But then this was in keeping with a tradition of more unexpected versions of the ZX: from the ZX 8000 Lego to the ZX 10000 *The Simpsons* 'Krusty Burger'; from the ZX 7000 HEYTEA with the Chinese tea chain of the same name to the ZX 8000 Meissen with Europe's oldest manufacturer of porcelain.

A Note on Jacques Chassaing

If Nike's designers would become recognized names in their own right – courting publicity and winning design prizes – Adidas would largely pursue a more collective ethos, a team effort that refused to highlight the contribution of any one individual. The one exception to this might be Jacques Chassaing.

The Alsace-born Chassaing started his career as a designer of dress footwear before joining Adidas France in 1981. He went on to guide the design of many of Adidas's signature shoes, among them the Forum (the upscale basketball boot that Adidas dared to release at twice the price of a pair Air Jordans), Rivalry, Stefan Edberg, Zelda, Lendl and Predator, as well as the EQT and ZX lines and collaborations with Porsche Design.

'To succeed as a designer you must be unique in your opinions, in your attitude and in your designs.'

'The 1980s was such an innovative time. There was an escalation with everyone trying to find something new. Everyone was taking a very technical, engineered approach because it was really all about running shoes,' the designer said at an END. Clothing event in 2019. He would go on to become head of Adidas Footwear Design International in 1993, and from 1998 would be head of Adidas Advanced Design Worldwide. 'Today the priority is much more on lifestyle sneakers. We didn't even call them sneakers back then.'

Chassaing's design ethos would prove hugely influential. Three years before Nike's Tinker Hatfield made the company's Air technology visible with the Air Max 1, Chassaing had in effect pursued the same design philosophy with the Forum when it was launched at the Los Angeles Olympics in 1984. Designed to integrate into the shoe the same support of the foot that basketball players would seek through strapping their feet, the Forum's distinctive leather cross-piece at the ankle made the construction clear for all to see.

'The thought process at the time was [that] when you wanted to introduce an innovative feature on a shoe, you should put it on the outside instead of hiding it within the construction,' Chassaing explained at a Footpatrol event in 2018. 'You can try to tell the consumer about what you have built on the inside of a product, but it was much more impactful to show it.' It's the same reason his favourite rendition of the ZX was the 2020 collaboration with Lego: the appearance of Lego explains how it works.

As for Chassaing's advice to his fellow sports shoe designers? At the same event, he said: 'Design must respond to issues, whether in sport or in everyday life,' he has said. 'To succeed as a designer you must be unique in your opinions, in your attitude and in your designs. Facing failures with the consumer is part of the game. You have to learn from it.'

Yeezy Boost 350

Kanye West's relationship with Adidas may have been shorter than was planned, but it nonetheless produced at least one style that helped define a decade, proving to be his most successful contribution to the Adidas portfolio. Maybe this was the style that would help Adidas, as West put it, 'jump over Jumpman' – a reference to his former employer's Jordan brand and its logo. Maybe it had been a long time in gestation: West had first worked with Adidas back in 2006, when he had proposed a reworking of its Rod Laver model of 1970, which was never made.

West dubbed the Boost 350 the 'Roshe Killer' – a jibe at the recently launched Nike Roshe sneaker, said to be inspired by designs he'd once proposed for Nike, and for which he would now not be receiving royalties. It was a highly technical shoe, its Primeknit upper and Boost cushioning making it extremely comfortable. But this running style also looked different, not just in being a low-top when fashion was drawn to hi-tops, and not just for its sock-like fit.

Rather, far from relying on bold graphics, overlays or colour, the first edition, released in 2015, came in a shade called 'turtle dove', an abstract, low-key

BELOW: Yeezy Boost 350 V2.

pattern in black and light grey. The next three editions, released later the same year, came in 'pirate black' (almost entirely black, relying on the Primeknit's textured surface for visual interest), 'moon rock' (taupe with erratic flecks of agate grey) and 'Oxford tan'. The 350 was minimalist when so many other shoe designs shouted.

There were variations, of course, including one with a translucent midsole and another with a studded outsole – as worn by the NFL Houston Texans wide receiver DeAndre Hopkins, winning him a US$6,000 fine. Why? Because the shoes didn't have a solid base colour. But if West's Yeezy 750 – his first official sneaker for Adidas, also released in 2015 – was a more challenging look, being a hi-top with full suede upper, cross-strap and full-length zip fastening, with the 350 he seemed to be onto something hugely commercial. It was taking all of the technical benefits Adidas had to offer and adding them to a highly wearable stripped-back shape and earthy colours.

Later versions might add a single broad stripe and/or the lettering 'SPLV' (said to stand, somewhat cryptically, for 'Saint Pablo Loves You', perhaps a reference to West's second child and his 2016 *The Life of Pablo* album). But they remained largely

RIGHT: Stormzy performing at Glastonbury wearing Yeezy Boost 350s.

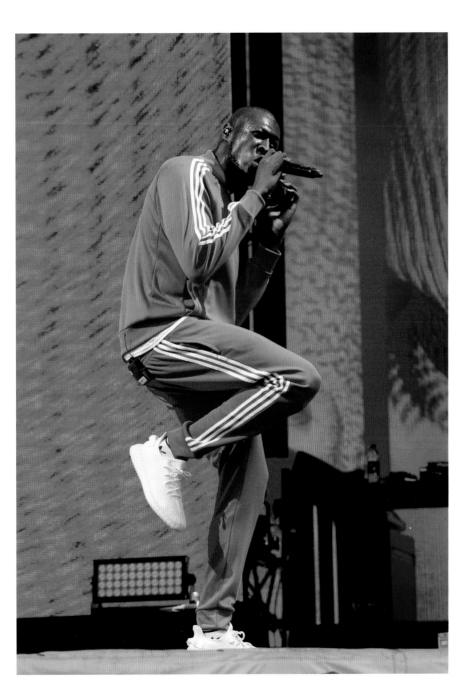

muted too. One of the style's most popular releases was in 'triple white'. 'These things,' West said of his shoe designs, 'are made to bring incalculable joy.' Sales suggested they did so.

Had it not been for West's wayward public comments and Adidas feeling it had to consequently terminate his contract (see pages 56–63), the 350 would have remained the linchpin of the musician's intention to build – with Adidas – an empire on footwear royalties, much as Michael Jordan had done with Nike. Only, so it was reported, West was getting three times Jordan's royalty. And West owns his own brand.

Kobe Bryant/Crazy 8

Kobe Bryant was just 17 when the future LA Lakers basketball superstar was signed by Adidas in 1996. The sports shoe company would back him in a big way too, offering him US$48 million over six seasons. But what impressive seasons those were, seeing Bryant win the Slam Dunk contest, appear in four All-Star games, win three NBA titles and, of course, launch a signature shoe line.

The Bryant deal gave Adidas a place in basketball it would later parlay into deals with other stars-in-the-making such as Tracy McGrady and James Harden. And although Bryant's relationship with Adidas would eventually sour over creative differences – with Bryant buying out his contract to flirt for a year with Jordan, Reebok and Converse, before finally signing with Nike – by then Adidas and Bryant had released a trio of show-stopping basketball boots.

Kobe would begin his contract with Adidas wearing the brand's Top Ten 2000, Top Ten 2010 and EQT Elevation, the latter in a fetching shade of purple. But in 1997 he got his own boot, the James Carnes-designed KB8 or Crazy 8. The black leather-and-suede style, with bold cloud-white abstract sidewall pattern and Feet You Wear tech (see pages 148–151), made a lasting impression: it would be rereleased as a period-correct replica in 2023. That tech also meant Bryant had to wear Adidas's Forum 2000 for half a season, after Frampton Ellis (the inventor of Feet You Wear) and Adidas found themselves in a court battle over its use, during which Adidas had to pause – and, finally, terminate – Feet You Wear altogether (when a settlement was reached in 2003 permanently ending the licence).

Bryant would soon move on from the KB8 and its various renditions in dramatic form. The shoe released in 2000, and dubbed simply the Kobe, could hardly have been more different. It was a clean-lined boot designed by Eirik Lund Nielsen with Peter Moore (designer of Nike's Air Jordan), and inspired by one of Bryant's favourite cars, Audi's TT Roadster. The connection is clear when the shoe is seen in profile.

Nielsen took the streamlining further still with the sculptural Kobe 2 the following year, arguably Adidas's most progressive basketball boot ever and, like a car prototype, one that even started out as a clay model. With Adidas's three-bar branding just about peeking from the sole, the super-minimalist, space-age shoe was free of decoration, excepting a special 'USA Flag' edition Bryant wore as a mark of respect following the terrorist attacks of 11 September 2001.

Perhaps the design was, in retrospect, too futuristic, as Bryant is said to have not liked it as much as he should have liked something carrying his name. Indeed, when playing he would often prefer to wear the Kobe 1. That, and the similarly avant-garde Kobe 3, which only made it to sample stage, may have been the breaking point in his partnership with Adidas.

LEFT: Kobe Bryant competing for the Los Angeles Lakers in 1998.

Technology

Adidas was once described as a technology company that just happens to work with sporting goods. As Adidas vice president of global design Nic Galway would point out in a 2015 interview with *Complex*: 'Everything [in an Adidas shoe] has a function. [Its parts] are not decorative. Everything is there for a reason, and if you were to remove [any] one element [of a design] it wouldn't work. It's really integrating, to give a result that's familiar but completely new.'

That Adidas was at least as much a tech company as a manufacturer of footwear was a point the company itself would eventually make implicitly in 1990, with the launch of its Equipment (EQT) line. Recognizing that its sales were increasingly going to people who did not wear their shoes for the intended purpose, Equipment put clear water between those products with 'style potential', and those of a more no-nonsense, performance-driven bent. But by then the company's history was already littered with one engineering or material innovation after another.

RIGHT: Adidas shoes being made in the Adidas factory in Herzogenaurach.

Football

It is perhaps little surprise that, while the Dassler brothers' business made its mark in the development of track shoes (the idea that sports footwear might be worn by the general public was a long way ahead), the newly formed Adidas company made inroads with other specialist products, specifically for the football (soccer) pitch.

Football was fast becoming an obsession in West Germany, its fans all too ready to mythologize the successes of the national team, on its way to becoming dominant in international competition. Hence what came to be known as the Wunder von Bern, or the Miracle of Bern, at the World Cup Final in 1954. West Germany was to play Hungary, both the favourites and the team that, earlier in the competition, had humiliated West Germany with an 8–3 defeat. But this time the German side would wear Adidas Argentina football boots.

As with the innovation that Dassler brought to spikes (see page 12), so studs would receive the same attention. Historically, football boots were ankle-height and heavyweight. Dassler gave the semi-professional West German team a more form-fitting, low-cut style that, although twice the price of orthodox football boots, was half the weight and

RIGHT: Footballer David Beckham wearing Adidas. Adidas and football have been closely affiliated from the beginning.

also featured a soft toe, foam-rubber interior and studs that could be swapped out for those best suited to the pitch conditions on the day.

Hungary took a 2–0 lead. In what football pundits would come to see as one of the greatest matches in World Cup history, West Germany changed their studs at half-time – switching to longer ones capable of sliding in and cleanly out of the turf, without collecting heavy mud on the sole of the boot – and fought back to win 3–2. 'What a Dassler!' as the headline in the UK's *Daily Sketch* would put it.

The World Cup of 1954 also happened to be the first to be televised. West Germany's victory not only cemented Adidas's place in the public consciousness, both at home and abroad, but also in the manufacture of football equipment. This would open the door to further technical advances. In 1958 Adidas's Der Weltmeister (World Champion) was the first soccer boot to use a sole made of polyamide, which allowed it to retain its shape in wet conditions. In 1966 its Achilles model introduced a heel-lacing system, and in 1979 the Copa Mundial came with foam cushioning that minimized the pressure of cleats underfoot. The Copa Mundial would subsequently become the boot of choice for many professional players for a generation.

Until, that is, Adidas reinvented the football boot again. If boots traditionally had a smooth surface,

to minimize disruption that bumps or seams might cause in contact with the ball, Adidas turned that thinking on its head. The Predator boot, launched in 1994, put a ripple of fins over the toe that, it was discovered, actually gave the player better control. Adidas promised that the Predator delivered '90 per cent more swerve and 10 per cent more power.'

Incidentally, it wasn't just with footwear that Adidas contributed to football. From 1963 it would start to make footballs. Indeed, if the popular conception of a soccer ball is of one comprising multiple pentagonal panels in black and white, this design – called the Telstar – was created by Adidas for the Mexico World Cup in 1970. This was in order to make the ball more visible for those audiences watching at home on black-and-white televisions (as most would be until the 1980s).

It would be the start of a long relationship with FIFA, the International Federation of Association Football, such that Adidas would go on to supply match balls

ABOVE: The ripples on the Predator facilitated better ball control.

for every World Cup that followed. As with boots, so the tech in balls would keep moving forwards too: in 2018 Adidas introduced the Telstar 18, a smooth, virtually seamless ball that would be described as a nightmare for goalkeepers to get a grip of.

Yet Adidas's more high-profile technological leaps truly resonated in the kind of sports shoes that could be worn, unlike football boots, in a more everyday setting. Not all the ideas Adidas pursued worked brilliantly, but they were always a testament to the spirit of innovation. Take, for example, 1984's Micropacer running shoe, which – in another first of its kind – incorporated a stat-tracking system into a tiny sleeve over the laces. This, it's important to note, was at a time when a mobile phone was literally the size of a brick.

'What I really loved about the products of the mid-80s was it was a time when the future was "the thing",' Nic Galway said to *Complex* in 2015. 'No one had computers at home [then. Yet] we, as a German brand, were making this wearable technology. It showed a really great pioneering spirit that [the company] must have had at that time.'

Cushioning

Maximizing cushioning, without adding weight, was a major concern for any manufacturer of sports

LEFT: Footballer Daniel Jeandupeux with the Telstar in 1973.

footwear. But the desired level of cushioning was also a matter of individual preference. To address this, in 1984 Adidas introduced the first cushioning system that could be customized: a peg system, built into the sole of the LA Trainer, and later the Grand Slam tennis shoe, and stiffened to more or less of a degree. The idea was further developed two years later with the APS running shoe, which built cushioning rods into the sole – rods that could then by hardened or softened using an accompanying key. Adiprene, another proprietary system, brought extra cushioning to the heel and forepart of some Adidas shoes, making them ideal for high-impact sport.

Innovative though such ideas were, they paled in comparison with Adidas's later technological breakthroughs in cushioning. In 2006 it introduced Bounce, a suspension-based system that, importantly, had the aesthetic appeal of Nike's visible Air, which gave shoe sole units a spring-like reaction. 'Returns energy with every step,' suggested one commercial for Bounce, though actually it is more the case that much less of the athlete's kinetic output is lost than otherwise would be. It certainly seemed to work: the Kenyan runner Patrick Makau, for instance, would set the world marathon record in Berlin in 2011 wearing a pair of Adios 2s with Bounce technology. Unfortunately, Adidas was unable to persuade more amateur runners to adopt Bounce, especially those in the US, the key market for runners.

That's one reason why, seven years later, Bounce was trounced by an even more sophisticated form of Adidas cushioning. Boost was devised in cooperation with the German chemical company BASF in 2012. It had created what it called 'energy capsules', thermoplastic polyurethane (TPU) pellets that, it later realized, found a use when they were fixed together into a solid piece. In order to demonstrate its springy qualities, BASF first tried this by making a tennis ball-sized ball from the pellets.

'Returns energy with every step.'

As Matthias Amm, category director in Adidas's Global Running division, would put it when he saw the ball in action, 'we could not believe how much higher the ball bounced back compared to ethyl vinyl acetate (EVA) foams, which were the standard material of the time. We imagined what we could do with that material – we could revolutionize the running industry [with it].'

Effectively, in melding 2,000 of these pellets together to form a sole unit, the springy sum of these parts was more than the whole. Unlike many EVA foam-based cushioning systems, the pellets also retained their shape and function over time. There was another benefit too: Boost was not only better than

Bounce, it was also cheaper to make, affording high profit margins on many of the shoes with which it would be used.

Again, like Bounce, Boost would prove itself in the field. First appearing in the Adidas Energy Boost shoe in 2013, the following year both men's and women's gold medals in the New York Marathon went to athletes wearing Boost, while one of them, Mary Keitany, would in 2017 set a new women's marathon world record in a pair of Adizero Adios Boosts. Indeed, while Adidas was benefitting from business moves such as reissuing the Stan Smith and signing a design collaboration with Kanye West, the launch of Boost was said to have turned around the fortunes of the entire company. It finally provided it with a technological advantage over Nike.

But also, an advantage in cool. Boost's aesthetic would appeal to those who barely ran for a bus: the streamlining and comfort that Boost afforded running shoes would be integral to designs like the Ultraboost,

RIGHT: The Adidas Energy Boost 3.

NMD and the Yeezy Boost 350, all of which were hits with fashion consumers. Pre-Boost, few people were wearing running shoes as a style statement.

Boost's aesthetic would appeal to those who barely ran for a bus.

When Kanye West was spotted wearing a pair of all-white Energy Boost ESM shoes and then, a few days later, a pair of the all-white Ultraboost – both well ahead of the launch of his own Adidas Yeezy products – Boost was given all the cachet it needed. When the rapper used Boost in his own designs for Adidas, its credibility was assured. Boost, arguably, was largely responsible for taking Adidas from a global revenue of US$19 billion in 2014, to US$23 billion just three years later.

Andy Barr, Adidas's Director of Global Creation, would say that 'until Boost there was no reason for someone to choose Adidas over our competitors. Most people [now] say that Boost is the reason they've taken notice of us.' The advent of Boost finally allowed Adidas to let go of its overreliance on its classics of yesteryear.

Materials

The new millennium may have kick-started a new fascination with, and development of, wonder materials with undreamt of, maybe revolutionary, functional properties. Adidas was no small part of this buzz of excitement.

Wicking systems, for example, have long been a consideration for outerwear: how to seal the body from the outside elements while also pulling off the seeming contradiction of letting out moisture and heat produced by the body. Adidas would ponder the same issue for its footwear, and in 2002 launched its Climacool system, applying special fibres to the upper, drawing heat up and out of the shoe, and a perforation to the mid- and outsole to allow for airflow under the athlete's foot. Likewise, in 2011 it launched SprintWeb, a supportive synthetic layer that backs onto the breathable mesh used in many of Adidas's performance shoes of the time, such as basketball star Derrick Rose's Crazy Light shoes.

But these would prove to be just the precursor to arguably Adidas's biggest materials innovation to date: Primeknit, launched to coincide with the London 2012 Olympics in the shape of the Adizero Primeknit shoe. Admittedly, Primeknit – a system by which, instead of stitching pieces of material together to make an upper, it is knitted in one seamless piece – was not quite first. Nike's similar Flyknit had been launched earlier the same year – in fact, Nike even unsuccessfully sued Adidas for copyright infringement.

All the same, Adidas would find its own edge, using a fused yarn that allowed it to digitally fine-tune the amount of flexibility or stability required at different parts of the upper. Just as importantly, the upper would be durable, extremely lightweight and provide a close, sock-like fit. Since it could be dyed, it opened up all sorts of creative possibilities to the look of shoes too, something that would, in time, be most graphically exploited in collaborative models with Missoni and in Pharrell Williams' Humanrace Sichona sneakers.

Indeed, the whole idea was one that Adidas had been thinking about ever since its textiles technicians had visited the Techtextil trade fair in Frankfurt in 2010 and come across a glove that was knitted with what were hailed as 'thermoplastic fuse yarns'. Coincidentally, Adidas had at the time engaged a number of industrial designers to think of ideas for future sports shoes – working on the basis that shoe

BELOW: Adidas's Climacool system.

ABOVE: Primeknit is used on the NMD.

design specialists inevitably get stuck in the same way of thinking – and one, Alexander Taylor, had proposed a shoe knitted from just such a material.

Producing such a shoe would not be easy, not least because the manufacturing methods were outside of Adidas's sphere of expertise. It took meetings with a number of flat-knit experts outside the company to begin to understand what the production of Primeknit at scale would entail. Yet, working with a number of specialist machine makers in Germany,

RIGHT: Jessica Ennis wore six pairs of Adidas shoes at the 2012 Olympic Games for the seven events that make up the heptathlon.

Adidas managed to get its Primeknit to market in just two years.

Adidas soon came to realize the untapped potential of the process. It wasn't just that there was much less wastage in knitting, as opposed to cutting-and-sewing an upper. Such a knitted material could, of course, be used for apparel, as Adidas later would in everything from sports bras to outdoor jackets under its Terrex hiking sub-brand. But, in allowing tension to be applied at different parts of the upper, it also meant Adidas could do away with laces on some footwear models.

That might be little more than a convenience. But, taking the Adidas brand back to its origins, on football boots the absence of laces was a real benefit to better ball control. In 2014 the company had already launched the world's first knitted football boot, the Samba Primeknit, its knit engineered so that different parts of the boot gave more or less friction between the foot and the ball. Nonetheless, one of Adidas's sponsored players, Mesut Özil, had the same year mentioned to the sports brand how frustrating he still found the necessity of knotting his laces over and over and then tucking in the ends, just to get them out of the way.

In doing away with laces on a knitted upper, Adidas had to develop an internal support system – also knitted – built in to anchor the foot in place. Enter, in

2016, the Ace 16+ PureControl boot, the first laceless knitted football boot. Özil finally had, by his own account, 'my dream product'.

Construction

But Adidas would also recognize that just making its shoes comfortable would not work for athletes unless the foot was also held properly in place. That matter was addressed in 1988 with Torsion, a system that built a thermoplastic bridge under the mid foot of a shoe, adding support but also allowing for a more efficient heel to toe transition (important to serious runners). Torsion was added to Adidas's ZX line, for as much a stylistic hit as a functional one, and the likes of the Torsion Spectrum basketball boot. It was, as a 1989 commercial would put it, 'created with one thing in mind – winning. If you really want it, you can'. A more cryptic commercial for Torsion started with the image of a lion, then showed the tennis star Steffi Graf playing, and ended with her looking to camera and saying 'meow'.

That few sports shoes can perform as efficiently as the bare foot can, were it not for abrasive surfaces and the problem of impact, is an insight that has long shaped sports footwear manufacturers' intention to strip back their products as far as possible, while still having a shoe left to sell. Again, Adidas was at least a decade ahead of the industry's more widespread interest in so-called 'barefoot shoes'.

The company had not always spotted the opportunities that had come its way: the Air technology that had helped make Nike the world leader – soles incorporating sealed pockets of gas for cushioning – had been offered by its inventor to Adidas first. It turned him down. But when designer Frampton Ellis offered his innovation, a shoe that contoured the natural shape and movements of the foot, Adidas pounced: it acquired the licence in 1994 and, just two years later, what it had called 'barefootwear' was launched with a name change as Feet You Wear.

Adidas was at least a decade ahead of . . . so called 'barefoot shoes'.

Ellis had noticed that the 'squared off' soles of traditionally designed shoes were one of the most frequent causes of ankle rolls. What was required was a wider base and one lower to the ground, with a curve from outsole to midsole that provided lateral stability. Ellis calculated that with a conventional shoe you could land on the side of your foot at one-third of 1G and cause severe ankle pain; with his design you could land at 7Gs with none at all.

RIGHT: Stefi Graf at the US Open in 1996.

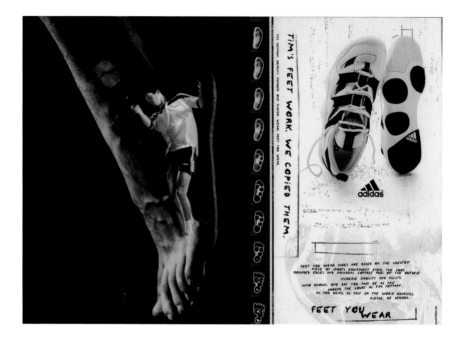

ABOVE: Feet You Wear ad from 1990s.

The technology was one of Adidas's bestselling, debuting with the KB9 III worn by Adidas ambassador Kobe Bryant ('Kobe's foot works. We copied it,' as one commercial boasted), with the Feet You Wear system also worn by Steffi Graf to win the 1996 US Open. Bryant, incidentally, had been signed to Adidas before he was even drafted by the LA Lakers, by one Sonny Vaccaro – the man who had convinced Nike to sign Michael Jordan in 1984 and was later fired by Nike too.

Adidas said it intended to put the technology in 90 per cent of the footwear it made, and certainly it shaped the look of many of the brand's key styles of the period, the Key Trainer and the Top Ten 2000 among them. That, at least, was the plan, had contracts not got in the way: Ellis and Adidas fell out over royalties, leading to a protracted legal case and, ultimately, the end of the license in 2003.

Perhaps this hard experience at least encouraged Adidas to think anew about construction. In 2016 it began working on a pioneering project, dubbed 4DFWD, which promised to completely rethink the way a shoe was put together and what it was put together from.

Indeed, most immediately striking about the likes of 2018's Alphaedge or 2019's ZX 4000 – the first of this new generation of shoes – was that they dispensed with the traditional foam midsole altogether. Instead, the midsole units were made from a 3D-printed lattice. It was developed using so-called 'Digital Light Synthesis' technology by a Silicon Valley company called Carbon; when compressed it responded by expanding forwards rather than upwards, so propelling the wearer forwards, akin to the carbon plates incorporated in soles, not without controversy, by other sports shoe makers.

But to this spectacular latticed sole would be added a new way of thinking about the upper too. Calling it Futurecraft.Strung was apt because everything about the idea would sound futuristic, not least that it involved uppers being made by custom-built robots working to a digital design to place over one thousand individual TPU-coated yarns at angles and layers calculated by some heavyweight computation. These threads came together to form the cocoon-like upper of a shoe. This would result in what Adidas would call a 'dynamic textile'; unlike most textiles, in which threads have to be placed in a hatched formation, crossing each other, often in a repeated pattern, Strung would allow the threads to be placed in a more chaotic fashion.

Chaotic, at least, to the eye. In fact, each thread would be 'tuned' to have different properties – varying degrees of tightness, for example, perhaps around the heel where more stiffness is usually needed – with variations in the tiny gaps between the threads also allowing for a textile of more or less flexibility or breathability. Crunching a lot of data about foot movements would allow Adidas to position each of the threads to maximum effect and in accordance with the function of each pair of shoes.

Unsurprisingly, when the first showcase shoe with both 4D midsole and Strung upper was revealed in late 2020, this radical design caused a sensation. Although, given the complexity of manufacturing and limited scope to scale it up, such a product was squarely aimed at very serious runners indeed (at least at the time of writing).

This was a market that Adidas had been in danger of losing almost entirely to Nike. But its technological accomplishments were, by this time, starting to bear fruit. In 2020 the Kenyan runner Peres Jepchirchir smashed the women's half marathon world record in Prague wearing a pair of Adizero Adios Pros. Instead of carbon fibre plates, by this time commonplace in pro-level running shoes, this design incorporated a series of curved carbon-infused rods, stiffened to carefully varying degrees and wedged between two panels of its Lightstrike Pro foam –

ABOVE: Futurecraft. Strung knitting robot.

a combination designed to mirror the metatarsal bones of the foot and said to give the shoe a more natural gait than the more standard carbon plate.

Scientific studies would be required to explain how such a shoe construction and its internal components increases running efficiency, and, to date, these haven't been done. Adidas would argue that it wasn't as simple as putting such a plate in a shoe. Rather, it was the subtle combination of various technologies, in the right quantities and with the right balance, that worked.

In 2023, Ethiopian Tigst Assefa won the Berlin Marathon, crushing the women's world record by over two minutes. She was wearing a super-light, 140g (4.9oz) pair of Adizero Adios Pro Evo 1s, shoes so finely tuned each pair would only be good for one race; shoes that their maker Adidas claimed, 'challenge the boundaries of racing'.

RIGHT: Tigst Assefa breaking the women's world marathon record in Berlin in 2023.

Epilogue

There is a scene in Ben Affleck's film *Air* (2023) – about the signing of Michael Jordan to Nike – that juxtaposes the free-wheeling spirit of the American company against the rigid corporate culture of Adidas, who were all suits around a boardroom table, apparently lacking the vision to see the opportunity in front of them. That's a good story to underpin the rivalry between the two sportswear giants. It's good for a movie.

But the truth is something else: Adidas, like Nike, has made mistakes, but arguably it is its very Germanic rigour and persistence that has seen it become one of very few companies to thrive for over a century, and do so by taking not one path but many: technicality but also heritage, sport but also fashion. Few companies would be able to embrace both designing and making footballs and designing and making drawstring lace-up high-heels. But if Adidas can see a rational case for pursuing the unexpected, it has been ready to do so.

In this Adidas has arguably transcended being the sporting goods brand that, perhaps, it still prefers to think of itself as. Rather, Adidas has become a cultural arbiter that just happens to make sporting goods.

Index

Picture Credits

Alamy

Action Plus Sports Images 22; adsR 77; Album 66, 67; Andrii Omelchenko 36-37; Associated Press 50, 58; Bill Waterson 27; Classic Picture Library 14; CN Photography 128; Cristian Storto 85; DedMityay 123; dpa picture alliance archive 24; Hugh Threlfall 143; Jack Carey 135; lev radin 60; PA Images 54, 82, 86, 125; Patti McConville 23; PCN Photography 28, 145, 149; Pictorial Press Ltd 65; Retro AdArchives 8-9, 13, 35bl, 35br, 35cl, 35cr, 35tl, 35tr, 150; Stephen Chung 153; Sueddeutsche Zeitung Photo 15; WENN Rights Ltd 40b, 40t; xMarshall 93, 112

Getty

Kevin Mazur 42; Christian Vierig 91; Daniele Venturelli 71; Dave Benett 119; David M. Benett 100; Duncan Raban/Popperfoto 75; Estrop 68; Focus On Sport 95; Frazer Harrison 106; Gary M. Prior 133; Gotham 79; Gregory Bojorquez 96; Janette Beckman 99; Jeremy Moeller 80, 81, 105; Lynn Goldsmith 108; Marvin Ibo Guengoer 155; Melodie Jeng 61; Mick Hutson 53, 57; Oliver Morris 45; Paul Popper/Popperfoto 21; Patrick PIEL 131; Raymond Hall 49; Sebastian Reuter 72; ullstein bild 10, 30, 136

Shutterstock

andersphoto 88; Duerr 144; Prestige Photography115; Steve Fenton 104; xMarshall 31, 102, 103, 109, 140

LAURENCE KING

First published in Great Britain in 2024 by
Laurence King
An imprint of Quercus Editions Ltd
Carmelite House
50 Victoria Embankment
London EC4Y 0DZ
An Hachette UK company

Text © Josh Sims

The moral right of Josh Sims to be identified as the author of this work has been asserted in accordance with the Copyright, Designs and Patents Act, 1988. All rights reserved. No part of this publication may be reproduced or transmitted in any form or by any means, electronic or mechanical, including photocopy, recording, or any information storage and retrieval system, without permission in writing from the publisher.

A CIP catalogue record for this book is available from the British Library

HB ISBN 9781529438680
Ebook ISBN 9781529438697

Quercus Editions Ltd hereby exclude all liability to the extent permitted by law for any errors or omissions in this book and for any loss, damage or expense (whether direct or indirect) suffered by a third party relying on any information contained in this book.

10 9 8 7 6 5 4 3 2 1

Cover design and art direction: Luke Bird
Design: Ginny Zeal
Commissioning editor: Nicole Thomas
Project manager and editor: Victoria Lympus
Printed and bound in Italy by L.E.G.O. S.p.A.

Papers used by Quercus are from well-managed forests and other responsible sources.